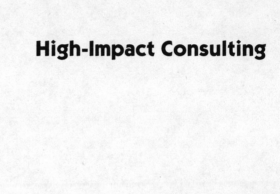

High-Impact Consulting

High-Impact Consulting

How Clients and Consultants
Can Leverage Rapid Results
into Long-Term Gains

Robert H. Schaffer

Jossey-Bass Publishers • San Francisco

Substantial discounts on bulk quantities of Jossey-Bass books are available to corporations, professional associations, and other organizations. For details and discount information, contact the special sales department at Jossey-Bass Inc., Publishers (415) 433–1740; Fax (800) 605–2665.

For sales outside the United States, please contact your local Simon & Schuster International Office.

Jossey-Bass Web address: http://www.josseybass.com

 Manufactured in the United States of America on Lyons Falls Turin Book. This paper is acid-free and 100 percent totally chlorine-free.

Library of Congress Cataloging-in-Publication Data

Schaffer, Robert H.
    High-impact consulting : how clients and consultants can leverage rapid results into long-term gains / Robert H. Schaffer.
        p. cm. — (Jossey-Bass business & management series)
    Includes bibliographical references and index.
    ISBN 0-7879-0341-8 (alk. paper)
    1. Business consultants. 2. Management. I. Title. II. Series.
HD69.C6S27 1997
001'.068—DC21   96-53432

FIRST EDITION
HB Printing   10 9 8 7 6 5 4 3 2

The Jossey-Bass
Business & Management Series

To my wife, Natalie

Contents

Preface

Most management consultants subscribe to a model of consulting that is inherently loaded against success. This consulting paradigm, followed throughout the world by external and staff consultants alike, is unnecessarily labor-intensive, long in cycle time, and low in return on investment. It locks both clients and consultants into a fundamentally ineffective mode of operation. In this, the conventional consulting model, there is a clear divide between the parties: The experts are accountable for creating the best possible solutions and tools, and the clients are accountable for exploiting those solutions and tools to improve organization results. In too many cases, however, clients do not or cannot implement the consultant-developed solutions in ways that yield significant improvement.

This book, addressed to senior managers and the consultants they hire or employ, describes a powerful, contrasting model: *high-impact consulting*. Over several decades a number of different consultants have demonstrated it to be highly effective in hundreds of applications. It has been employed in some of the world's most successful organizations, including General Electric, Motorola, General Reinsurance, Bell Canada, Northern Telecom, The World Bank, and Dun & Bradstreet.

Development of the New Paradigm

High-Impact Consulting has been almost thirty years in the making. In the late 1960s, the head of industrial engineering at Union Carbide asked me to lead a conference for his people. Every one of them possessed a toolbox full of techniques and methodologies that they were certain could help the company make significant improvements in costs, quality, and output. Yet many of the company's operations managers did not seem interested in receiving this help. And when projects were carried out, it was difficult to get the managers to make the changes necessary for them to benefit from the industrial engineering. Thus the engineers were able to achieve very little, despite the fact that they had identified huge opportunities for improvement.

Together the Union Carbide engineers and I worked on these issues in our conference, and shortly thereafter I published an American Management Association monograph called *Maximizing the Impact of Industrial Engineering*.[1] That conference and monograph marked the beginning of nearly thirty years of work on how consultants can best mobilize action in client organizations to improve their performance and accelerate the pace of change. My associates and I have applied the lessons learned along the way in our own consulting practice and in educating other consultants. With this book I hope to share this experience with a wider audience of managers and consultants.

In the intervening years the world has become much more complex. Change has become more rapid and pervasive. The management consulting profession has proliferated beyond anyone's wildest expectations. Yet despite all of this change, the dilemma faced by Union Carbide's industrial engineers almost thirty years ago remains the most significant issue confronting management consultants and their clients. Although the consulting profession has grown at an intoxicating pace, it has failed to solve its basic weakness, the difficulty of translating the consultant's skills and knowledge into successful change for the client.

It is important to note that I use *management consulting* here to refer to expertise aimed at helping organizations actually effect pos-

itive changes and improvements. One respected consultant told me
of submitting a report to a client who appreciated it but took
absolutely no action. The consultant maintained that the project
was nevertheless very valuable, because the client had learned much
about his business that he had not previously understood. Although
this result might represent a successful outsourced research project
(provided the client was looking only for insights rather than actual
change), in my view it signals a failure as a consulting project. Management consulting projects that do not yield demonstrably improved
client performance are as successful as books on weight reduction that
do not produce any weight loss in their readers.

My indictment of consulting grows from its failure to consis-
tently produce significant results. Responsibility for this situation
cannot be ascribed to consultant incompetence or avarice: the
overwhelming majority of consultants, I believe, are reasonably
competent in their fields and eager to do a decent job. Rather, consulting efforts usually founder on the shoals of various organizational obstacles, or they receive inadequate management support.
Thus consultants may expend substantial effort producing technically excellent reports that have little impact or installing superb
systems that yield little of value for the client.

If consulting contributes so little, why does it continue to grow
so rapidly?

- First, consulting projects are generally defined not in terms
  of client results but rather in terms of consulting products
  (the studies, recommendations, systems, and solutions the
  consultant will provide). Consultants have convinced most
  clients to accept as "success" the delivery of these products
  rather than the actual achievement of some measurable result.
  Thus, failures are effectively camouflaged.

- Second, there is the matter of need. Managers facing pressure
  to deal with rapid and complex change know that they need
  help, and consulting offers it to them in a form that is acceptable in the corporate world.

- Third, consultants do produce a certain number of genuine successes in which real and measurable improvements in client performance are realized, and they publicize these successes skillfully.

Consequently, many senior managers who need to improve their organization's performance call upon management consultants simply because they have won broad acceptability, no matter how poor their actual record of results. Hiring a consultant almost always seems to be better than doing nothing.

Throughout this book, I cite many examples of companies' actual experiences with management consultants. Where successful episodes are described and the parties have given permission, they are identified. Since it is not my purpose to criticize any specific individuals, all failures are presented without identifying the participants. (I did not follow this rule, however, in the case of material that has already been published.)

To write on this subject it is necessary to make broad generalizations, and I have certainly done so in criticizing conventional consulting. I do recognize, however, that a number of consulting firms and individual consultants have attempted to deal with the issues I raise in this book. While I name only a few of them here, there are a number of others who have enjoyed varying degrees of success. The best way to deal with the generalizations in this book is to use an "if the shoe fits" approach. Clients and consultants can consider their own experiences and decide what, if anything, they must to do to make their client-consultant relationships more effective.

Who Should Read This Book and Why

Clients of internal consulting groups and of outside management consulting firms should read this book. They will see that they may be deluding themselves if they share the widespread belief that if only they invest enough in the services of knowledgeable consultants they will be reasonably certain to benefit. This book explains why most clients are probably not getting the results they deserve, how they may be contributing to this state of affairs themselves, and what they can do differently (and ask their consultants to do differently) to ensure significantly better results.

This book will help managers see that their faith in the power of consultants' solutions, although frequently misplaced, is widely shared, not only in management circles but also in many other spheres of life. It will describe the price managers and organizations pay for perpetuating the traditional consulting paradigm—for succumbing to the illusion of "the expert's" power—and it describes the role managers must play in increasing the odds of success.

Of course, this book is also addressed to all management consultants, whether or not "consultant" is in their job title. To me, you are a management consultant if your job is to apply unique knowledge, skills, insights, methods, or technology to help managers get better results, and you lack any direct authority to require those managers to follow your advice. The book will be of particular interest to those professionals who want to become more effective change agents—those who feel that they are functioning too much as management technologists or high-level contract labor. The book's goal is to have management consultants measure their worth not only by the excellence of their solutions and recommendations but also by how much continuing benefit their clients derive from their input.

Finally, the book speaks to internal consultants and to corporate staff groups charged with improving performance, including finance, human resources and organization development, information technology, operations, logistics and inventory, and strategic planning professionals. Many books on management consulting exclude these groups and focus exclusively on consulting firms. But, in fact, there are many more internal management consultants than members of consulting firms. If you fit the definition given above, then you are a management consultant, and this book is for you.

Stamford, Connecticut   Robert H. Schaffer
January 1997

Acknowledgments

In this book I emphasize that it is just as important for management consultants to learn from their clients as it is for clients to learn from their consultants. As one who has put this concept into practice during my professional career, I wish to acknowledge the wealth of learning I have garnered from the people in organizations I have worked with over the years. To them I offer my profound thanks and appreciation.

Many of the concepts presented in this book have been the subject of case conferences and informal discussions with my colleagues at Robert H. Schaffer & Associates, and I am most appreciative to them for stimulating my thinking and helping me hone my ideas. They have also provided abundant case material and counsel on the book as it developed. They include Ron Ashkenas, Regan Backer, Harlow Cohen, Nick Craig, Suzanne Francis, Claude Guay, Rick Heinick, Elaine Mandrish, Keith Michaelson, Matthew McCreight, Nadim Matta, Robert Neiman, Rudi Siddik, and Harvey Thomson.

I also benefited from case material and generously shared personal recollections from Tom Barron, Mike Berkin, Charles Baum, Rodney Blanckenberg, David Francis, Bob Gunn, Tom Kivlehan, Bob Moore, and Doug Smith.

Geoffrey Love of Rice University provided extensive help in editing the manuscript. He and Katherine Paul-Chowdhury of

Western Ontario University also gathered case material from both clients and consultants and carried out other research tasks.

Joanne Young provided administrative support that helped me keep my consulting and managerial jobs going while I wrote the book, and Emilieanne Koehnlein assisted with the intricacies of graphics and manuscript preparation.

R.H.S.

The Author

Robert H. Schaffer founded Robert H. Schaffer & Associates and has been its head for over thirty years. Schaffer is the originator of the firm's unique results-driven approach, described in his 1988 book *The Breakthrough Strategy: Using Short-Term Successes to Build the High Performance Organization* (New York: HarperBusiness, 1988). The firm employs this strategy to help organizations achieve major performance improvement and accelerate the pace of change.

The firm has worked with such clients as AlliedSignal, Chase Manhattan Bank, Fidelity Investments, General Electric, General Reinsurance, IBM, Morgan Guaranty Trust, Motorola, Northern Telecom, the World Bank, and many other companies, as well as a number of government and social agencies.

Schaffer holds a bachelor's degree in engineering and a doctorate in counseling and management psychology, both from Columbia University. He has played a leadership role in the consulting profession as a founding director of the Institute of Management Consultants and as chairman of its Professional Development Committee for four years. He helped to launch the *Journal of Management Consulting* and has served as an editor for many years. He inaugurated and continues to manage "Consulting for Results," the longest-running workshop for management consultants.

Two of Schaffer's articles made the *Harvard Business Review*'s "best-seller" list for the early 1990s. One of these, "Demand Better

Results—And Get Them," was first published in 1974 and then republished as a *Harvard Business Review* Classic in 1991. The other was "Successful Change Programs Begin with Results," published in the January-February 1992 issue. He is also the author of three other *Harvard Business Review* articles as well as numerous other articles in a variety of journals on productivity, change management, and management consulting.

Robert Schaffer may be reached at:

Robert H. Schaffer & Associates
4 High Ridge Park
Stamford, CT 06905–1325
(203) 322–1604
e-mail address: rhschaffer@rhsa.com

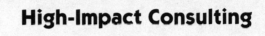

High-Impact Consulting

PART ONE

Why Management Consulting Fails and How It Can Succeed

1
___

Low-Yield, Conventional Consulting versus High-Yield, High-Impact Consulting

What constitutes success in management consulting? To help answer this question in the seminars I give for consultants, I always share the following story. It captures in the most simple terms imaginable one of the most profound issues in management consulting.

A family who had been unhappy for many years about the messy state of various storage spaces in their house read about a firm of "closet consultants." After a hasty phone call from the family, the consultants arrived on the scene to provide a free preliminary survey. Shortly a proposal arrived by mail, outlining what the consultants would do with the master bedroom closet. The family initialed the agreement, and within two weeks a miracle was wrought. New equipment was installed, and everything in the closet was tastefully, even artistically, arranged. It was a pleasure for the family to witness the transformation, and they willingly paid the consultants' fees. It was a happy ending, except . . .

Within three or four weeks, the closet was just about as messy as it had been before the consulting project. Except for the fixtures that had been screwed into the wall, there was little by which to remember the project.

The closet consultants exercised their professional skills and delivered a superb solution. Yet, although it exactly met the client's stated requirements, the "solution" failed to yield sustained value for the client. Was the consulting project successful? The answer to this question is important, because a great many management consulting projects have the same sort of outcome. Consultants frequently labor long and diligently to produce technically excellent solutions that fail to produce the results desired by their client.

Consider, for example, the experience of one global corporation:

A consulting firm was retained by the corporate headquarters of a large global company to study the marketing approach of a particularly powerful competitor and to develop an effective counterstrategy. Five divisions of the client company were to be involved.

The consultants began by interviewing a number of senior executives in the client company. They learned about the unique operations, goals, and strategies of each of the five divisions included in the project. They then conducted extensive research in many different marketplaces to gather information on the competitor.

The consultants prepared a thorough analysis of the threats posed by the competitor and offered a fairly detailed menu of possible counterstrategies for dealing with them. Although they had performed a first-rate analysis and produced some excellent solutions, when they tried to convene a strategy summit of the general managers of the affected divisions to discuss an action plan, they could not make it happen. No real action was ever taken on the report. Despite this fact, the corporate officers who had hired the consultants were very impressed with the high quality of their professional work and judged the project a success.

A success? We disagree. The elegant and creative recommendations prepared for the managers of the global corporation failed to advance the company's competitive position one iota, just as the closet consultant's efforts failed to improve the client family's lifestyle. Any solution—no matter how creative—that provides no benefits for the client is, in my view, a failure. Unfortunately, such "solutions" are prolific in management consulting.

Success in Consulting

I reject the rationalization that many consultants offer, that such projects are technically successful since the consultants have provided the "right answers," but for some reason—undoubtedly various client shortcomings—the clients were unable to benefit from the projects. "Right answers" that do not help clients achieve what they are trying to achieve are, in fact, wrong answers.

For a management consulting project to be called a success, three outcomes must be achieved.

- First, the consultant must provide a solution or a method new to the client.

- Second, the client must achieve some measurable improvement in its results by adopting the consultant's solution.

- Third, the client must be able to sustain the improvement over time.

In other words, management consultants must be more than experts in their field. They must serve as effective change agents and share accountability with their clients for the ultimate outcome of their consulting projects.

Most consultants are willing to be held to the first success criterion only, but not the second and third. While they always hope that their clients will achieve sustainable bottom-line benefits from their input, few consultants agree to be held accountable for client outcomes. The reason is that conventional consulting is based on the assumption that consultants' principal value comes from their expertise, from their ability to make flawless recommendations or to install powerful new processes or systems. Consultants concentrate on making sure that their recommendations are "professionally correct." They pay much less attention to their clients' capacity to actually *benefit* from their recommendations.

Here is where both clients and consultants fail to recognize the fundamental flaw of the conventional approach: like Sunday sermons, parental advice, diet books, and doctors' admonitions about smoking and obesity, conventional consulting is based on the assumption that the key to progress is greater knowledge. In other words, once the client knows what to do, then the client will achieve greater success.

But real-world experience suggests that this is a false assumption. Mountains of data indicate that only rarely is not knowing what to do the greatest obstacle to organizational success. Much more often it is not being able to do it. Who would say that in the 1930s and 1940s Packard Motors, Studebaker, and Willys-Overland did not have the same market information and were not trying to pursue the same strategies that enabled General Motors, Ford, and Chrysler to succeed? And who would say that in the 1960s and 1970s General Motors, Ford, and Chrysler were not privy to all the information they needed to prevail over their Japanese competitors? They simply lacked the capacity to translate their insights into effective action.

Despite the occasional victories that come from knowing which horse to bet on, more often the key to business success is the ability to effectively translate insights and ideas into needed change. The ultimate value of consulting inputs always depends on the ability of the client organization to absorb and use them to achieve better results. As people have known for thousands of years, even the best advice often fails to produce an iota of progress.

Flawed Assumptions, Flawed Designs

The design of most consulting projects reflects the flawed assumptions of conventional consulting. Most are virtually completely dedicated to providing managers with insights and ideas *about* change but pay virtually no attention to helping the client *effect* change. In fact, client limitations in this area are generally not viewed as an appropriate focus for the consultant's attention. Rather, they are viewed as hazards to the practice of consulting, like sand traps on a golf course. Over and over again, I hear consultants complain about organizational barriers that prevent their clients from achieving good results from their recommendations—almost as if it were unfair to have to deal with these obstacles.

For example, a consultant-developed sales forecasting system fails because the sales force does not provide the required data and support. A corporation implements a consultant's recommendations for organizational restructuring but places the wrong people in some key roles. A client rejects a carefully developed marketing plan because it contradicts the CEO's beliefs. A company sets aside a major strategy study because it calls for directional shifts too radical for senior management to risk. Such occurrences are quite common, and when they occur, discouraged management consultants usually blame the disappointing results on psychological, cultural, or other limitations of the client organization. They never see that the very design of their consulting project contained the seeds of its failure.

Consultants will thoroughly research a client's problems but pay virtually no attention to assessing the client's willingness and ability to implement the suggestions that the consultants might make to solve those problems. Consultants usually find out what their clients are able to do with their recommendations only after the consulting project is over and their recommendations are already made. By then it is often too late.

Also, consultants usually assume that the best way to attack any subject—whether cash flow, marketing strategy, or inventory turns—is to examine it in its totality. Consultants almost always want to produce a "big-picture" solution; anything less is considered piecemeal or suboptimizing. But large-scale studies usually take very long, are very costly, and result in change plans that are much too complex for most organizations to carry out.

Further, consulting projects are usually considered to be mainly within the province of the consultant. Consultants do their work and then hand over the result to their clients. The clients, with little opportunity to develop their own insights or the skills needed to implement the recommended changes—and busy with all the other aspects of their jobs—are nevertheless expected to be able to implement the consultants' recommendations.

These are only a few of the self-defeating design features of conventional consulting. It is no wonder that a significant number of projects directed by highly knowledgeable and motivated consultants produce great ideas, great reports, powerful new systems and methods, but little or no real benefit for the client. This has been accepted as the essential nature of the management consulting game. To improve their batting average, consultants have experimented with new techniques and have paid greater attention to implementation issues. But neither consultants nor their clients have questioned the fundamental paradigm of conventional management consulting. And that is where the solution lies, not in fixes and adjustments, but in some basic shifts in the way management consulting is practiced.

The High-Impact Paradigm

High-impact consulting is based on the premise that although the consultant's expert solutions are vital to the success of a consulting project, it is just as vital for consultants to help clients absorb, use, and benefit from those solutions. Merely dishing up the consulting "products" with the assumption that the client can "take it from there" makes each project a gamble—and a poor one at that. Client success must be carefully designed into the process. And client success must include client learning and development.

In order to ensure success, each project should be constructed to produce a plan that the client is apt to be ready, willing, and able to implement. If the client can, with a bit of effort, run five miles, why design a project that will require him or her to run a twenty-six-mile marathon? Also, instead of tackling a huge project all at once, the client and consultant can carve off subprojects, each focused on a near-term goal that both parties are reasonably certain can be achieved. These first subprojects can provide the reinforcement of success. They can provide experience that proves helpful in subsequent projects, laying a foundation for continuing, expanding cycles of success.

High-impact consultants devote as much energy to helping their clients develop the necessary skills and confidence as they do to their technical studies. As clients experience success in the early phases of the process, they develop new skills and confidence that help them in the overall change effort. They gradually develop the ability to attack increasingly ambitious undertakings.

These fundamental shifts, the essence of the high-impact paradigm, take much of the gamble out of consulting. Because the strategy is designed to mobilize and exploit the client's own capabilities and to overcome the organizational barriers that often sabotage improvement, it can significantly increase clients' return on their investments in consulting.

It is not very difficult for managers and consultants to make these shifts. Any who are ready to try it will be surprised by the results they get and the ease with which they get them. The difficult part is wrenching yourself psychologically from the conventional model, an approach that has for so long provided a cozy security blanket for so many managers and consultants. The essence of this shift to high-impact consulting is that consultants will no longer regard the attainment of measurable bottom-line results and the sustaining of those results by the client merely as desirable outcomes of consulting projects—these will be essential goals of virtually all consulting projects and the criteria for evaluating their success, as important as developing the right solution or installing the right process.

2

The Five Fatal Flaws of Conventional Consulting

In the 1980s, Quotom Supply (a disguised name) was the dominant office equipment and supply distributor in a large region of the United States. They ran a number of retail stores and a mail order operation and served large companies through a well-organized sales force. And they were making money in all of these businesses. In 1987, the company's managers decided that it would be worthwhile trying to figure out how to make this extremely successful enterprise even more successful. They engaged a highly competent, well-known consulting firm to do an "opportunity identification study." The firm did the study and developed several dozen possibilities for expanding into new business areas. They were highly creative ideas, and any of them, if actually implemented, might well have been successful.

None of the suggestions was followed, however. It was not that the managers were dissatisfied with the recommendations. They had asked the consultants to do a piece of work, and the consultants had done what they were asked to do. The managers affirmed that it had been done well, but they were simply not ready or willing to implement any of the suggested solutions.

By 1989 the situation had changed. A large national distributor had begun to move into Quotom Supply's region.

This competitor could undercut Quotom prices because of its greater bargaining power with manufacturers and also because it owned a number of its manufacturing facilities.

Quotom Supply's market share dropped significantly. The same consulting firm that did the earlier opportunity identification study was invited to help the company's management regain its market position. As a senior associate of the firm described it,

We did a classic consulting strategy study. It encompassed understanding the economics, understanding the marketplace, including the supply chain, including customers and the key competitor, and understanding the role of the distribution channels.

We developed many new insights about the economics of the business. We discovered that there were significant differences in what various categories of customers felt were the most important value factors for them. We discovered that many of the services Quotom Supply felt they had to provide to all their customers were useless to certain groups of them. We discovered that Quotom was in a position to provide certain unique customer-by-customer services that the large national competitor couldn't possibly provide.

We developed a set of recommendations for carefully segmenting their market, then reorganizing the operations of each of their units to reflect the unique needs of the segments they were serving.

While we were doing our study, an opportunity arose for testing our concepts. One of Quotom's largest customers was threatening to shift much of its business to the national competitor. We convinced management to experiment with the new tailor-made response service we were going to propose. They tried it, and the customer was pleased and did not shift to the competitor.

When we finally came up with our full array of recommendations, the heads of Quotom accepted them, and they put them into effect quickly and efficiently. As a result, the downward market share trend reversed. Within three years, in fact, the company was able to increase their market share by about 35 percent even though the national competitor continued to expand in Quotom's region.

Success Is Elusive

Here was a consulting project that netted tens of millions of dollars for the client. Yet just a few years previously, an equally competent consulting team had completed a project for the same client that produced virtually nothing. In the later, successful, case, the client was driven by a sense of urgency. Management had to get moving quickly. The consultant team's recommendations were clear and easy for the client to carry out, and they were validated along the way with a pilot effort. Finally, the consultants provided a solution that matched what the company's salespeople had been asking for.

In the earlier project, there was no similar sense of urgency and no opportunity to test the consultants' directions along the way. To implement their recommendations would have required the client's managers to venture into risky new territory where they had little experience or confidence.

Effective action ensued only when the consultants' recommendations were aligned with the client's motivation and skills. In the earlier project, where the client's motivations were not in alignment with the consultant's recommendations, there was no successful action.

Most consultants regard the risk of such misalignment as an unavoidable aspect of management consulting, a risk for which they cannot be held responsible. They mainly feel responsible for making sure that they conduct the necessary studies and provide the correct solutions and insights. Unfortunately, clients' capabilities and motivations frequently are not well aligned with their consultants' recommendations. While clients can win big, as in the successful Quotom case, clients frequently fail to win at all.

Some Evidence of the Problem

The available evidence suggests that the results in the earlier Quotom case are more typical than those in the later, successful project. Consider some of the most common change programs of the last decade. In the late 1980s and early 1990s, one of the most popular consulting products was Total Quality Management (TQM), in all its variations. The American Electronics Association conducted a survey in 1991 of TQM efforts at high-technology companies. Of the more than three hundred companies that responded, most reported an active TQM program under way. Of those, two-thirds reported that they had been able to reduce defects by only 10 percent or less.[1]

Similarly, an article in *The Economist* reported on a survey by Arthur D. Little of five hundred manufacturing and service companies.[2] Of these, only a third felt that their total quality programs were having a "significant impact." The article also quoted a study by A. T. Kearney of over one hundred British firms. Only a fifth of those companies believed that their quality programs had achieved tangible improvements. A number of other studies reported similar findings.

In the 1990s, reengineering replaced TQM as the most popular consulting product. As with TQM, the published evidence is bleak. Gene Hall, Jim Rosenthal, and Judy Wade reported in the *Harvard Business Review* on reengineering programs in over one hundred corporations.[3] They noted that in most of the companies the efforts produced some process improvements but little, if any, improvement in overall business results. And even James Champy, one of the movement's founders, reports that "even substantial reengineering payoffs appear to have fallen well short of potential."[4]

In 1994 *Consultants News* reported that "Business Process Reengineering, the current darling of American management, is having a good run, with consultants, academic devotees and the business press all pushing it. Realistically, it's no different than dozens of other fads that have preceded it, and it's following the same life cycle." This was accompanied by a chart of over fifty fads, under the heading "Management's Field of Dreams, Headstones in Management's Graveyard: 50+ Fads and Panaceas in 50+ Years."[5]

The short life cycle of various management fads—the principle consulting "products" of the past three decades—further demonstrates the low success rate of conventional consulting. The cover story of the January 1986 *Business Week*, "Business Fads: What's In and Out," traced the evolution of magic management cures from the 1950s (Theory Y, management by objectives) to the 1980s (Theory Z, culture change, restructuring). The article asserted that these approaches "quickly become meaningless buzzwords, hollow symbols and mere fads."[6] Nitin Nohria, of Harvard Business School, and J. D. Berkley reached the same conclusion in 1994: "In the majority of cases, research shows, the management fads of the last 15 years rarely produced the promised results."[7] Most of these fads have been mainstays of consulting practice.

My own personal experience confirms these conclusions. For more than twenty-five years I have served as a consultant to management consulting firms and internal staff consulting groups. I have attended consulting conferences, conducted consulting seminars, observed consulting firms at work in dozens of client organizations, and talked with hundreds of managers who have worked with consulting firms and internal consulting groups. I helped launch the Institute of Management Consultants, served on its board, and served as an editor of the *Journal of Management Consulting*. These experiences have all provided insights into how consulting is practiced and the results it produces.

Key Obstacles to Consulting Success

Unquestionably, management consultants are motivated by a strong desire to make a useful contribution to their client organizations. Their goal is to introduce changes that will help their clients achieve their purposes more effectively. Yet, every consultant faces the dilemma faced by our closet consultants in Chapter One. The habits and lifestyle of the family that hired the consultants simply did not support the wonderful new closet arrangement that the consultants introduced. It was this mismatch between what the clients were willing and capable of doing and what the consultants' solution required of them that ultimately resulted in failure. In planning the closet project, the consultants did not consider the family's habits and its willingness to change them. Yet these factors were critical to the outcome of the assignment.

Management consultants must deal with similar dynamics every day. They deliver ideas for improved operations, new systems, better information, and new processes for achieving results. But in order for those to be successful, members of the client organization must change their work patterns enough to be able to adopt and support the innovations.

The operational patterns of an organization, however, are just as intractable as the lifestyle and personal habits of a family, and they are much more complex to understand and influence.

Any number of obstacles may need to be overcome in order to change an organization effectively. There may be impermeable barriers between organizational levels or between the organization and its suppliers and customers. Organizational departments and functions may be worlds unto themselves. The organization's managers may have weak performance expectations, accepting minimal effort from employees. Or they might allow employees all sorts of escape hatches when challenging goals are not being met. There may be meager rewards for outstanding performance and no adverse consequences for poor performance. Goals may be vague or unmeasurable. Accountability may be ambiguous. Change may induce a crisis mode rather than being a routine part of organizational life. Anxiety avoidance may result in unproductive behavior. This is just a sampling of the patterns that can undermine a consulting project. These and other obstacles are outlined in Exhibit 2.1.

EXHIBIT 2.1. Organizational Obstacles That Derail Consulting Projects.

1. **Psychological Myopia**
   - Feeling we are "doing the best we can"
   - Denying or distorting reality
   - Assuming time will solve the problems
   - Avoiding risk and commitment
2. **Wasteful Work Patterns**
   - Following old, familiar routines
   - Being "too busy" to be thoughtful
   - Impulsively trying one thing, then another
   - Overlooking the views of others
3. **Weak Performance Expectations**
   - Having overly modest goals
   - Leaving escape hatches for those who miss goals
   - Valuing explanations as highly as results
   - Providing no real consequences for performance levels
4. **Defective Work Management**
   - Having too many goals
   - Having vague or unmeasurable goals
   - Lacking clear accountability
   - Having weak or nonexistent work plans
   - Conducting infrequent or ineffectual progress reviews
5. **Cultural Barriers**
   - Allowing confused decision-making processes
   - Letting change become a crisis, not a routine
   - Having low expectations
   - Letting each unit go its own way

Most conventional consultants, highly sophisticated in their areas of expertise (such as business strategy, manufacturing methodology, information technology, and so on), are woefully naive about dealing with the psychological, cultural, and other organizational issues outlined in Exhibit 2.1. The basic consulting methods of almost all conventional firms, including those that feature "change management" practices, fail dismally to address these issues, even though over 90 percent of consulting failures and dis-appointments stem from them. In fact, the very design of the conventional consulting paradigm ignores these issues and thus dooms many consulting projects to failure.

The Five Fatal Flaws of Conventional Consulting

Whoever the client is, whatever the consultant's area of expertise, and regardless of whether an outside or staff consultant does the work, the conventional consulting process proceeds more or less in the same time-honored fashion:

- First, a manager describes the client's need to the consultant.
- Responsibility for the project shifts to the consultant, who takes over and prepares a proposal outlining the work that his or her team will perform and the consulting products they will produce.
- Once the client gives the go-ahead, the consultants carry out their work: researching the problem, conducting interviews, analyzing the organization, designing new systems, developing new processes or recommendations for change.
- Once the consultants have delivered their recommendations or completed the new systems specified in their proposal, they are considered to have fulfilled their commitment. Now it is the client's responsibility to exploit the consultant's products and (with or without additional consulting support) achieve the improvements that were the client's initial goal, the reason for hiring the consultant.

This pattern has five intrinsic characteristics that I refer to as the "frequently fatal flaws." Each of these flaws contributes to failure rather than success. Not every conventional consulting project is marked by all five flaws, but even three or four can block the path to success. The five flaws are as follows:

1.   *The project is defined in terms of the consultant's expertise or products, not in terms of specific client results to be achieved.* No matter what goals the client may have in mind when engaging a consultant, it is unlikely that the consulting project will be defined in terms of achieving those goals. Rather, the project will be defined in terms of the work the consultant will do and the products the consultant will deliver. Of course, the assumption always is that the consultant's deliverables will eventually be translated into the client's desired results. But that is only an assumption; it is rarely part of the contract.

Some examples will show how this happens:

- A rapidly growing electronics manufacturer, its inventories and accounts receivable burgeoning, is strapped for cash. Senior management identifies one urgent goal: *reduce inventories by significant amounts.* A consultant is hired to help. The consultant's project is defined as follows: *develop specifications for an improved inventory control system, and then design and install that system.* The consultant makes no commitment to help the client actually reduce specific categories of inventory by a specific percentage by a specific date.

- A chain of retail stores is enjoying healthy growth, but major changes in the marketplace are producing some significant competitive pressures. Senior officers decide that store managers need to *increase sales volume per employee.* A consultant is called in to help, and a project is defined as follows: *train store managers to enable them to better provide the leadership required to boost store sales volumes and profitability.* Even though the words "boost store sales volumes and profitability" are included in the project definition, a careful reading makes it clear that the goal to which the consultant has committed himself or herself is the training of store managers, not the boosting of sales volumes and profitability.

By defining projects in this way, clients allow consultants to avoid accountability for measurable performance results. The consultant is responsible only for delivering a product—a report, a system, business intelligence, strategic recommendations, or some other output that the consultant knows he or she is capable of delivering—rather than for delivering tangible results.

2.   *The project's scope is determined solely by the subject to be studied or the problem to be solved, ignoring the client's readiness for change.* When consultants are asked to recommend changes to some aspect of a client's organization, they begin by focusing on the system or process they have been asked to deal with: How is it working now? What is working well? What is not working well? How do the elements fit together? What might a changed or improved system look like? Such questions result in projects that are almost always designed completely around the subject to be studied, the problem to be solved, or the system to be installed, with the assumption that the consultant, applying his or her expertise in a particular area, will uncover the best way to handle it. Rarely do consultants, in designing a project, consider questions like these: What kind of changes might we recommend at the completion of this study? How likely is it that our client will want to carry out those recommendations? Will the client be capable of making those changes successfully? Only at the end of a project, when the consultants are ready to make their recommendations, do the client's motivations and capabilities suddenly become a matter of concern. At that point, dozens of factors hindering implementation might suddenly become apparent, thwarting the success of even the most competently designed solution.

Here is an illustration of what often happens:

A large national financial services company had always sold its products and services through a network of regional offices with an employee sales force. Several senior officers thought that if the national company could sell directly to the consumer and eliminate regional offices and a full-time sales force, there was great potential for enhanced growth and earnings. To make this decision, they needed to better understand their customers' motivations: How did they feel about the company's products and services? How did they view the competition? And how would they respond to alternative sales methods? They invited a consulting firm, well known for its strategy work, to provide the information needed to decide for or against eliminating the regional sales forces and to develop an overall market strategy for the next five years.

Because of the complexity of the assignment and the rather large stakes, the consultant invested several months in designing a project proposal that would encompass all of the relevant factors. A very thorough, comprehensive plan was outlined, reviewed with the client, and then carried out.

The work took over eighteen months to complete. The major consulting activity consisted of data gathering and detailed analyses of the national economy, the company's competition, and its customers' attitudes. As many as a dozen consultants at a time worked on the project, and it cost the client several millions of dollars.

At the end of the project, a number of volumes of the consultants' findings and recommendations were prepared. There was a formal presentation to senior management. The major findings were summarized, and a rather creative new strategy for the company was offered. At this presentation, management suddenly understood the enormity of the effort required to transform the company and also the risks that would be involved in doing so. The potential gains suddenly paled by comparison. After a few more sessions to explore the strategy in greater detail, the consultants were paid and the project terminated.

The consultants conducted a thorough, competent study and devised a creative plan to accomplish what the client said it wanted to do. The consultants' recommended changes were much too radical and risky for the company's management, however. Since the consultants made no analysis at the beginning of the project of what their client might be willing and able to implement, they spent many months and millions of dollars generating sound, imaginative recommendations that never had a chance of being implemented. This happens all the time.

3.   *The project aims for one big solution rather than incremental successes*. The financial services company may well have been willing to take some more modest steps to test some of the ideas and assumptions underlying the consultants' comprehensive recommendations. Such steps were not considered or integrated into the project, however. Why? Once a need or problem is defined by the client, most consultants are geared to studying it in its totality and offering a complete remedy. The aim is to go as far as possible toward having the problem completely diagnosed and solved or a complete new system in place at the end of the project. This stems from the view of the consultant as a heavy hitter who provides answers and solutions but somehow is not responsible for execution.

This all-at-once, one-big-solution mentality reinforces the second fatal flaw. Projects are generally seen as an all-or-nothing process, with the consultant expected to study as much as possible of the issue at hand and arrive at the most complete solution possible. The client might actually be more willing or able to tackle a single element of the solution, but that is not discovered because the consultant is attuned to developing an overall solution that addresses the larger concepts involved.

Another negative result of this flaw is that many projects end up taking many months from the time they begin until the consultant delivers his or her recommendations and the client attempts to implement them. While a consulting project inches forward, month after month, adhering more or less to its original design, the organization moves on. The external world continues to change. Management priorities shift. Management personnel may change. All of these shifts affect what might work. Yet, like a glacier moving down the mountain, the project grinds forward toward its predetermined destiny.

When it is all over, both client and consultant can look back and think of many things that might have been done to make the project more useful. But by then it is too late—the time and resources have already been spent.

4.   *The project entails a sharp division of responsibility between client and consultant; there is no partnership between them.* In the financial services example, once the client identified its need and accepted the consulting firm's proposal, the consultants took over and went to work. The consultants conducted hundreds of interviews and discussed them informally with one another, developing some important insights into the buying patterns of their client company's customers. They clarified the nature of the relationships between various kinds of customers and the company's salespeople. They uncovered a number of serious problems. They devised a number of possible solutions and explored each of them thoroughly. Eventually, they narrowed their solutions down to a few possibilities that seemed very exciting to them. But none of the client company's people were directly involved in this creative process. Of course, the consultants did present occasional progress reports—but listening to progress reports is not the same as talking to customers and brainstorming options. By the end of the project the consultant team had coalesced around a set of well-conceived concepts, in which they had real confidence, but to the client their recommendations were all very new and very strange.

This illustrates the fourth fatal flaw, the sharp division of responsibilities between clients and consultants. In a conventional consulting relationship, project responsibilities are handed off, back and forth, between consultant and client. The financial services company case shows how the consultant's and client's perspectives can diverge as a project progresses. While client managers go blithely on with their daily routines, the consultants are exposed to a wealth of data that the client never sees. As a consequence, the consultant may develop a strikingly different point of view on the project.

There are other risks in the back-and-forth hand-off mode: certain managers with strong views on the subject under study may not be consulted during the project. Individuals who will have to play a key role in implementing the consultant's recommendations may be similarly ignored.

These are all time bombs waiting to go off at the end of a project. The more work the consultant carries out without close client involvement and the longer the cycle time from start to finish, the greater the likelihood of missed connections, of recommendations that call for actions that are much too complex for the client to comprehend or carry out.

The hand-off choreography of consulting projects is similar to the way new products used to be developed. First, a company's marketing or sales department would identify a consumer need. Then, with a project authorization in hand, Engineering or R&D would begin developing the new product. They would then go back to Marketing and present their tentative designs. Marketing would react, and then the technical people would go do their part again. Finally, after Marketing and R&D agreed on the product design, it would be taken to Manufacturing. Manufacturing would study the drawings and announce what elements of the design could or could not be manufactured. In response, the plans would be modified. Perhaps the plans would have to go back to Marketing for approval of the design changes. Then Manufacturing would estimate the cost of the product. And so it would go, until a few years later when the product would arrive in the marketplace.

Most companies have learned that new products can be developed in a fraction of the time and at a fraction of the cost if they are developed by teams representing all of the key functions, working together throughout the process. But few consultants have experimented with replacing the hand-off mode of consulting with a more effective, collaborative mode.

5. *The project makes labor-intensive use of consultants, instead of leveraged use.* In the case of the financial services company, a team of twelve consultants worked for over eighteen months to develop a comprehensive but indigestible set of recommendations. Such labor-intensive use of consultants illustrates the fifth flaw of conventional consulting.

This flaw is the virtually inevitable consequence of the other four flaws. When the goal of a project is to arrive at "the best answer," and the client and consultants agree that this will require a comprehensive study, and it is understood that the consultants will do the bulk of the work, then it is not surprising if the project involves a large group of consultants working long hours. When consultants work on project tasks by themselves, without transferring knowledge to client personnel and without engaging client personnel in the work of the project, that is the essence of labor-intensive consulting. It overlooks the gains that are possible if consulting effort is leveraged by having client people learn from the consultants and take over increasing amounts of the work of the project. Some cynics point to consultants' economic incentive in heavily staffing a project. While that may be part of it, the entire structure of conventional consulting leads inevitably to a labor-intensive mode of operation.

Many consulting firms and internal consultants recognize that this is not a good way to work. They may even make some attempts to get their clients involved in project work. The great majority of consultants, however, seem to be unwilling or unable to depart from the conventional, labor-intensive consulting model.

Not all five flaws afflict every consulting project. In most conventional firms, however, enough projects are affected by enough of the flaws that many clients receive no significant benefit. Moreover, the longer a project, the more organizational units it affects, and the more different programs it introduces, the more likely it will fail. Take the case of this fairly large project in a health insurance company, carried out by a well-known, respected consulting firm:

The company had a serious problem with falling profits. It needed to significantly reduce its expenses and improve the effectiveness of its operations. Even though the company's senior managers were not clear on the strategic direction the company should take, they did agree that expenses had to be cut by about 20 percent. The head of the consulting firm promised the company's president that a comprehensive reengineering project could accomplish that goal.

The consultants selected a group of about forty company employees and twenty-five consultants, most of them relatively new MBAs. This group was divided into process redesign teams to study six primary processes, with many subteams organized around related processes.

The assessment and redesign activities of these various teams went on for about a year. Although senior managers were given periodic progress reports, they were not really encouraged to become active in the project. They were expected to listen and approve. Similarly, company personnel serving on the teams quickly discovered that the consultants incorporated only those ideas that they viewed as acceptable.

At the end of the redesign phase, the consultants presented the company's senior managers with voluminous documents containing more information than any of them could absorb. The consultants' plan called for all sorts of radical work-process and related changes, to be carried out more or less simultaneously at headquarters and in the field. Various offices were to be consolidated, moved, or redesigned. The company's products and services were to undergo fundamental shifts. The company was to reduce its staff. And all of this was supposed to be carried out by a management team that had little experience in implementing change.

The company tried to implement a few of the consultants' recommendations, but the effort soon bogged down. The net effect was that the business was worse off than it had been before.

This was a typical conventional consulting project: the client wanted to reduce its expenses, and after a year it received a complicated *plan* to do so but no actual reductions. The consultants' plan gave no consideration to the client's ability to implement change, nor was this capability developed one iota during the year-long project. The project followed the characteristic labor-intensive, one-big-solution model. After a year of work and untold millions of dollars of direct and indirect expenses, the consultants had not tested a single redesign recommendation to see if their plan would actually work for their client. All five fatal flaws (summarized in Exhibit 2.2) were honed to a fine edge by this large, well-respected consulting firm, which as you read these words has hundreds of consultants out repeating this flawed pattern with other clients.

Most of the books and articles on consulting take for granted the conventional, big-picture, one-time-around, lengthy and labor-intensive consulting model. When such an effort works, it can produce fantastic results. When the moon and stars and planets are all in alignment and the consultant's recommendations mobilize effective client action, there can be some powerful outcomes, outcomes that the client could never have achieved on its own.

The evidence suggests, however, that such successes are more the exception than the rule. Dozens of things can go wrong, and these things are not typically controlled within the framework of the conventional model. It is much more common for the moon, stars, and planets not to align. High-impact consulting offers an alternative for clients who want more assurance of success than the conventional model provides and for the consultants who want to provide it.

EXHIBIT 2.2. The Five Fatal Flaws of Conventional Consulting.

1. Project defined in terms of consultant's products (not in terms of client results to be achieved)
2. Project scope based on subject matter logic (not on client readiness for change)
3. One big solution (rather than incremental successes)
4. Hand-offs back and forth (instead of client-consultant partnerships)
5. Labor-intensive use of consultants (instead of leveraged use)

3

The Bottom-Line Results
of High-Impact Consulting

During the 1930s, one of President Franklin Roosevelt's top priorities was to revive the country's ailing agricultural sector. Thousands of "county agents" were deployed by the Department of Agriculture to provide education and consultation to farmers. One such agent in western Nebraska encountered a farmer who had not made use of this assistance. After some small talk, the agent said, "Say, Calvin, how about if I come by next week to see if I can be of some help?" "Thanks very much," Calvin responded, "but you needn't bother to visit. I ain't farmin' half as good as I already know how to farm."

Calvin's self-awareness was exceptional, but his situation is similar to that of many senior managers. Most already know what their organization should be doing differently; they simply are not capable of making it happen. For every manager I have encountered who was in the dark about what strategic direction to pursue, I have met twenty or thirty who knew what they wanted to do but were frustrated by not being able to do it fast enough or well enough.

The ability to make things happen, to effect change, is thus the most critical dimension of organizational success. A new management tool or a strategic vision can be created in a relatively short time by a few bright people. To significantly enhance an organization's performance and capacity for change, however, requires very hard work by many people over a number of years. As Professor Arthur Turner of the Harvard Business School put it, in a more sophisticated expression of Calvin's insightful remark, "It is often easier, but less useful, to transmit to a client a valid diagnosis of what is wrong and what should be done about it, than to interact with members of the client organization in such a way that the things which 'should' happen actually come to pass."[1]

As we have seen, the conventional consulting paradigm is not designed to mobilize organizational change. High-impact consulting, by contrast, focuses on implementing solutions as much as on discovering them. It is explicitly designed to produce *all three* elements of consulting success: expert recommendations, bottom-line results, and client capacity to sustain improvements. Indeed, high-impact consulting aims to expand the skills, confidence, and enthusiasm of the client to go even further. It is designed to help the Calvins of the world to farm as well as they know how to farm, and then to learn even more.

Here's an example of high-impact consulting in action:

The United Aluminum Corporation, a rolling and processing mill in Connecticut, invested large sums over a five-year period in technical consulting and in installing the rolling-mill control equipment the consultant recommended. The resulting productivity gains were only a few percentage points a year, however.

A colleague of mine, Keith Michaelson, collaborated with an internal consultant at the company to address the need for greater productivity. A small group of mill operators and supervisors were invited to help the company capture greater benefits from its investment by further increasing the rolling mill's throughput.

In a series of brainstorming sessions, the consultants tuned in to the participants' resistance to improvement as well as to the participants' ideas for achieving it. The consultants encouraged senior management to respond to a number of "hidden agenda" items that surfaced.

Once management had met with the team of mill personnel and dealt with a number of their questions, the group agreed to shoot for a 15 percent gain in six weeks. The team ran the project. It was made very clear—by word and deed—that the consultants were there to provide methodological help as needed but were not "in charge" of the project. All members of the team were encouraged to contribute their ideas. By the end of the six weeks, productivity had actually increased by 17 percent—five or six times the amount gained over the previous several years. And this level was not only sustained in subsequent years but actually increased to higher levels, again without further capital investment.

THE NEXT STEP

At around this same time, company management decided to take action to improve their on-time shipment record, which was down around 80 percent. They were about to engage a consultant to recommend and install an order-tracking system, at a cost of about $2 million.

The company's experience in the rolling-mill productivity project suggested that a purely technical solution might not solve the late shipments problem. So the company postponed the systems study and asked Michaelson to help them shoot for some rapid results on the on-time shipments problem.

In collaboration with several internal consultants, Michaelson proposed and then helped carry out the following pilot project, without making any changes in the information system. The mill managers agreed to try, with some consulting assistance, to ship 100 percent of orders out during a one-week experiment by "doing everything right." One month of preparation was scheduled before the trial week. The managers were not asked to commit to maintaining that level of service after the one-week experiment. Employees in every department were asked to help prepare for the experiment, and everyone's ideas were welcomed.

During the one-week pilot (and the following week, too) every single order was shipped on time. Thereafter, delivery performance never fell below 95 percent. Some modest information-system improvements were needed to sustain the performance, but nothing like a $2 million system.

Reversing the Five Fatal Flaws

These two projects illustrate a consulting process that eliminates most of the risks of conventional consulting and adds dimensions that can multiply the benefits of management consulting many times. The approach sharply contrasts with conventional consulting because it reverses the five frequently fatal flaws of the conventional model, transmuting them into techniques that reduce risks and enhance returns:

1. Instead of defining projects in terms of the consultant's expertise or the products (solutions, reports, systems, and so on) the consultant will deliver, high-impact consulting *defines projects in terms of specific performance goals that will be attained*.

2. Instead of determining a project's scope in terms of the subject to be studied, high-impact consulting *determines projects' scope based on an assessment of what the client is likely to be willing and able to do*.

3. Instead of aiming for "one big solution" that will require a long cycle time and huge up-front investment, high-impact consulting *divides projects into increments, with rapid cycle times, for quicker results*.

4. Instead of passing responsibility back and forth between clients and consultants, high-impact consulting *encourages both parties to work and learn together, in full partnership mode, through every stage of the project*.

5. Instead of making labor-intensive use of teams of consultants, high-impact consulting *makes leveraged use of consulting inputs*.

By reversing each of the five frequently fatal flaws of conventional consulting, high-impact consulting creates a low-risk, rapid-return developmental process. Each project is designed not only to produce some tangible result but also to expand the capability of both client and consultant to tackle increasingly ambitious projects with increasing competence.

Tapping the Client's Latent Potential

High-impact consulting is based on the belief that fostering an organization's ability to implement change is the key to strengthening its fundamental capability. As our Nebraskan farmer, Calvin, knew well, there's no sense in giving more advice to someone who is already not doing half as much as he knows he should be doing.

How can consultants strengthen their clients' implementation capability? One important clue can be found in the fact that when a crisis or must-do situation suddenly arises, virtually every organization can spontaneously mobilize a response. Let the possibility of landing a new important account arise, or let a fire or flood occur, and suddenly there is a surge of effectiveness—as much as double or triple the normal level. All of us have seen many examples, in our own organizations or in events like these:

- Some years ago, an Exxon refinery with 2,800 employees (a number the plant's managers had complained was inadequate) was hit with a sudden wildcat strike. Unable to plan for a safe, orderly shutdown, the managers kept the refinery going, assuming the stoppage would be over quickly. Instead, it continued for months, while about 450 of its managers and engineers kept the refinery going at full capacity.

- In 1993, northern Georgia had a record snowfall of about fifteen inches. The roof over part of a Mohawk Carpet mill, unable to support the load, collapsed, destroying one of two production lines in a fully loaded factory. Within days, thanks to the inventiveness and dedication of the people in the mill, the remaining line was producing what both lines had been producing before the storm.

- A group of health insurance claims examiners whose productivity was low and whose work was fraught with errors was, as part of an experiment, offered time off if they reached some new levels of output. Within hours they increased their output by about 50 percent, and the error rate dropped.

- After the Chicago poisonings temporarily put them out of business in the early 1980s, Tylenol developed a triple safety packaging system and restarted production within three months, instead of the more normal twelve to eighteen months to develop such a system.

Every manager can cite similar "miracles" when fires, floods, or earthquakes occur or when sudden sales opportunities or client-imposed deadlines arise. It is obvious that none of these organizations' capability was "created" at the moment their crisis occurred. Consider that to achieve such dramatic improvements, an organization's people must modify their personal work patterns, shift their priorities, and reorganize their work processes, eliminating those of little value. That they can do it so fast and so well, and without any consulting help, means that they must already have possessed the know-how and capability.

To capture this potential every day, it is necessary to know what releases it in "must-do" situations. My associates and I have asked thousands of managers and consultants what they think is the answer to this question. They all responded quickly, and every group enumerated virtually the same list of causes. I call them the "zest factors," and they are listed in Exhibit 3.1.[2]

The more an undertaking is characterized by these zest factors, the more a group will mobilize its energies, overturn barriers, and set aside low-value-added activities. Consider some consulting projects you are familiar with and test them against the list. Most likely you will recall that the consultants had considerable zest for the project, but there was little or no zest on the part of the clients. Projects are rarely focused on a few critical results. Clients rarely feel they are working toward goals that are "clear, measurable, and short-term."

EXHIBIT 3.1. The Zest Factors.

- There is a focus on a few critical results.
- The goals are clear, measurable, and short-term.
- There is a real sense of urgency. It must be done.
- People see that success depends on them—and they assume the responsibility.
- People realize they must experiment to achieve their goals.

Nor do most consulting projects have a sense of urgency about them. It is no wonder, therefore, that most conventional consulting projects fail to mobilize the client's hidden potential.

Carving off and achieving a rapid-cycle results goal, however, does provide a sense of zest. There is a clear-cut focus. Clients feel a sense of responsibility; they are invited to be creative in devising and implementing solutions. From the first moment, both client and consultant are focused on identifying and implementing actions that will yield results quickly.

Achieving Success

Simply put, using high-impact consulting is like loading the dice for success. Each project is designed to exploit the untapped capabilities of the client, with the help of the consultants. Focusing on real results that have some urgency mobilizes people's energy. Designing rapid-cycle subprojects means people have a chance to see the results of their efforts quickly. Having clients work in partnership with the consultants encourages people to share their creative ideas and experiment.

Let's see how each of the five shifts from the conventional model to high-impact consulting contributes to liberating the client's untapped capability.

Focus on Results

Instead of being defined in terms of the work the consultants will perform and the products they will deliver, which is how virtually all consulting projects are defined, projects are defined in terms of measurable client results that client and consultant agree to achieve together. For example, suppose a company wants to speed the pace of new product development and hires a consultant to help. A high-impact consultant would define the project in terms of achieving actual reductions in the time to develop new products. If the client wants to enter a new market, the high-impact consultant's goal would be to help the client enter that market. If a company is experiencing errors and delays in processing orders, a high-impact consulting project would have the goal of reducing errors and delays by some specified amount within some specified period.

In each of those assignments, the consultants would contribute technical know-how and introduce new systems and work methods. But measurable results would have to be achieved for the project to be considered successful.

Many consultants, if asked whether they define projects in terms of client goals, would leap to their feet and assert that of course they do, for satisfying client goals are their only raison d'être. But, as mentioned in Chapter Two, a quick scan of one of their typical proposals would likely suggest otherwise. A proposal for an order-entry project, for example, might define the consultant's task as something like this: "Study the company's present order-processing system, identify needed improvements, and recommend and install new processes designed to reduce errors and eliminate delays in order processing." Although the project definition uses the words "reduce errors and eliminate delays," the consultants in fact have committed only to recommending and installing new processes that are *designed* to reduce errors, sometime in the future.

Many consultants (and clients) use the word *results* to mean almost any product of a consulting study. A truly results-focused definition of a consulting project needs to be very specific about the client's needs, however. In a semiconductor plant, for example, a quality project might be defined as follows: "In a joint undertaking, increase second-pass yields from the current 60 percent level to 80 percent or more within three months." With such a project definition in hand, client and consultant will both be focused on the same goals, and both will assess their success by the same criteria.

Of course the consultants will provide some expert input to help improve the targeted process or system, but providing that input won't *be* the project. Rather, those inputs will be but one contribution *to* the project made by the consultants along the way. The consultants, no matter how elegant their solutions, will not consider themselves successful unless tangible, measurable results are achieved—rejects are reduced or yields are improved, for example.

Focusing on a real, bottom-line result important to the client adds zest to any consulting project. Rather than being a distraction from the client's efforts to achieve a desired goal, the project *becomes* the effort. Such a focus generates more commitment than a consulting project that promises great results sometime in the distant future.

Certain types of projects may be more difficult to define in terms of concrete results. Strategic planning projects and major systems projects are examples. I will show in Chapter Four, however, how virtually every kind of consulting project can be translated into results-oriented terms.

Assess Client Motivation and Capability

In designing a consulting project, it is essential that the client and consultant, at the earliest possible moment, together assess what kinds of changes the client is likely to be ready, willing, and able to carry out. The project can then be designed so that the amount of change it eventually calls for will not extend far beyond that estimate.

A client exploring a new project with a consultant should insist on discussing the possible implications of the project in terms of the actions the consultant might recommend that the client take. The client and consultant should together consider what types of changes would likely be feasible.

Often when consultants are asked at the beginning of a project to speculate about its possible outcomes, they will hedge: "We can't predict what the recommendations might be until we do the study and get the results." In fact, though, any experienced consultant, even after only brief exposure to a new situation, should be able to provide a range of possible recommendations and outcomes. He or she certainly should be able to make some educated guesses. And clients should insist on hearing some of those guesses. Only when you have a sense of what your organization might have to do to benefit from a consultant's work can you reliably assess whether the project is a certain winner or needs to be redesigned.

As both client and consultant sharpen their sense of the client's readiness to act, they can carefully design (or redesign) the project so that their expectations for change will align with the organization's estimated capabilities. This process shifts the essential nature of a consulting project from a gamble to more of a sure bet.

Divide Large Projects into Rapid-Cycle Subprojects

The longer a project drags on, the less likely it will deliver the desired results. The client's needs (or how it views them) may change during the six or eight or twelve months a project is under way. Some of the key players in the organization may change jobs or priorities. Market and competitive conditions may shift. Time and again I have heard about large information-systems projects that cost many millions of dollars but had to be abandoned along the way or were completed but were not modified to meet the client's changing needs.

The most reliable and powerful way to minimize these risks is to carve off from the overall project a series of subprojects, each of which will yield some results and some success in a short period of time—five or six weeks, if possible, or three or four months. The first project at United Aluminum, for example, began producing major gains in six weeks. Here is another example:

An office machine distribution company engaged a consulting firm to help increase the productivity of its national sales force. Client and consultant both agreed on the general approach that would be used, but instead of trying to launch a change effort in all twelve of the company's branch offices, they decided to try it first in one branch. The branch selected for the trial was one whose manager had expressed some interest in receiving help to increase sales. Several interviews with personnel at that branch revealed that the most urgent need was to increase sales in the major account categories. After some further dialogue, a project was designed with the goal of increasing major account sales by $100,000 a month over a period of ten to twelve weeks.

By focusing intently on one goal, they succeeded. Equally important, both client and consultant learned something about what would work and what would not. They were able to sharpen the design of the project as they moved forward within the first branch and then on to the others.

Carving off rapid-cycle subprojects may be the single most important contributor to stimulating the zest factors in an organization. When there is a clear, short-term end result in sight, people can get enthused about making it happen. Since the goal is more contained, there is less at stake, so people feel freer to experiment. And as people enjoy some successes, their willingness to shoot for tougher goals expands.

Carving off shorter-term projects is not done at the expense of pursuing a more strategic vision. Managers who select rapid-cycle goals are asked to make certain that those goals align with the company's longer-term strategies. In fact, as each rapid-cycle project is carried out, one of its aims should be to gather and test more information about those longer-term strategies. Many far-reaching strategic change projects, such as the GE Workout process and the Motorola Organization Effectiveness Process, were constructed on a foundation of specific incremental achievements.

Develop a Partnership

Once a consulting project is aimed at achieving some targeted, measurable improvements in a relatively short period of time, the conventional consulting project's back-and-forth hand-offs of responsibility simply won't work. Clients and consultants must work together as partners, agreeing on what must be done, allocating tasks, and working together to achieve the desired results.

Suppose, for example, that a client wants to find out whether a new product is likely to succeed. The client and consultant might decide that instead of undertaking a massive study of the possible markets, they will collaborate on a real-time test of the product in one or two major markets. They discuss between themselves how the test might be carried out. Perhaps they obtain the views of other people in the organization. They now share a common, results-focused, rapid-cycle goal, a conviction that the goal is achievable, and a common view of how they will carry out the project.

One indication of the shift from conventional to high-impact consulting is that the project design statement is no longer prepared by the consultant and conveyed to the client. Since a high-impact consulting project is a collaborative process, it can only be described in a document that is prepared jointly.

The partnership relationship also makes each project a learning experience for both the client and the consultant. During each rapid-cycle subproject, the client's people learn how to identify a goal and achieve it. They learn how to use the consultant's expert inputs, adopt them, and put them to work. They also learn how to implement changes, how to get various groups to collaborate in carrying them out. Thus every project carried out in the high-impact mode yields management-development and organizational-development benefits for the client, as well as tangible bottom-line results.

The consultants learn too. In conventional consulting, the consultants are assumed to be the font of all knowledge and wisdom. Many consultants cultivate this aura of omniscience to prop up their professional image and self-confidence. But consultant learning is a key developmental building block of high-impact consulting. At the very least, the initial projects in an organization teach the consultants what it takes to make things happen in that organization.

One of the most important things that both client and consultant learn from following the high-impact model is how to proceed together to reach their goal. That is, as client and consultant work together on their first subproject, they gain insight into how they can best move forward with their collaboration. They share the task of identifying goals for the next step and the best way to move forward to achieve them. This is in contrast to the heavy dumps of material and recommendations at the end of a conventional consulting project, which often make clients plead with their consultants to "Please go away and give us a chance to absorb what you've already given us."

Thus the partnership mode kindles a sense of responsibility on the part of client staff. They are not just standing around answering the consultant's questions and waiting for the consultant to drop the final blueprint on them.

Leverage Consulting Inputs

If a consulting project is aimed at rapid-cycle, measurable results and the client and consultants are working together to make it happen, the amount of consulting hours necessary is greatly reduced compared to the typical labor-intensive conventional project. A principal objective of high-impact consulting is to help clients make better use of their own talents and skills. With this perspective, and with greater emphasis on achieving results and less on producing voluminous studies, consultants need do much less, because the client accomplishes so much more with what the consultant provides. That is why high-impact consulting is also high-leverage consulting.

A drastic reduction in costs is only one of the benefits of high-leverage consulting. At least as important is the implied message to everyone in the client organization that "This is our project, and we are the ones who will have to make it succeed, with the help of the consultants." The zest that is aroused by this sense of personal responsibility contrasts markedly with the malaise and cynicism that is aroused when twenty or thirty or fifty consultants are scampering around, poring over files, calling meetings, making notes, and so on.

As consultants and clients plan projects in ways that leverage the costly consulting inputs to maximum effectiveness, they will discover that small amounts of consultant input can go a long way when the client is prepared to absorb and use it.

So, as summarized in Exhibit 3.2, high-impact consulting takes the five frequently fatal flaws of conventional consulting and reverses them. The result is an entirely different way of looking at management consulting.

As the last chapter noted, not all conventional consultants are always completely locked into the five fatal flaws. Many have adopted elements of higher-leverage, results-focused strategies. I do not advocate that every consultant attempt to suddenly shift to the high-impact model on all five factors. Rather, consultants should experiment with adopting those high-impact consulting ideas that seem most compatible with their individual mode of practicing. I do, however, urge all clients to be unrelenting in their demand that consultants demonstrate their worth by producing measurable results in fairly short order.

Blending Content Consulting with Process Consulting

Many writers on the subject divide the consulting world into two sectors. Most consultants are "content consultants," functioning as experts on substantive issues such as information technology, logistics, manufacturing processes, strategy, finance, and so on. "Process consultants" offer help in determining how things should happen in an organization, but they don't devote much energy to content issues (or to achieving results).

It seems obvious that effective consulting as I have defined it requires a blend of content consulting with process consulting, with a strong added emphasis on achieving results. Arthur Turner advocated this shift in a 1983 paper entitled *Expert or Facilitator?* In it he describes the consulting process as a "collaboration between

EXHIBIT 3.2. Conventional Consulting versus High-Impact Consulting.

Conventional Consulting	High-Impact Consulting
1. Defining the project	
Project goals are defined in terms of the solutions, systems, recommendations, or techniques to be provided by the consultant.	Project goals are defined in terms of measurable improvements in clients' bottom-line results.
2. Determining the project's scope	
The project's scope is determined by the systems or technical issues to be studied.	The project's scope is determined by assessing what the client will be willing and able to absorb and implement.
3. Designing the project	
Projects are large scale, with long cycle times and the speed and maneuverability of a glacier.	Projects are divided into steps to produce rapid results and to gain the experience that enables further progress.
4. Working on the project	
First the client passes the problem to the consultant; then the consultant does the job and passes the results back to the client.	The client and consultant work together as partners at every stage of the project.
5. Deploying consultants	
Large consulting teams do the work, with little client involvement.	Consultants provide focused support to client teams, who take major responsibility for the project.
The Consequences	
Big up-front investments and long cycle times before value can be assessed; high risk and frequently low returns or unmeasurable returns; may be little or no client learning.	Low risk, high returns; consultant time highly leveraged; short cycle time, so there is little investment before seeing a payoff; client capabilities expand with each cycle.

consultant and client in discovering and mobilizing readiness for action to improve performance, [with the] desired outcome [of] more effective task accomplishment and relevant learning within the client organization."[3] In the paper, Turner quotes Carl Sloane, former head of Temple, Barker & Sloane and then professor at Harvard Business School, who wrote, "I have never seen an issue of any significance that is entirely substance or entirely process."[4] High-impact consulting offers a results-oriented framework for blending substance and process.

Change Is Long Overdue

Hundreds of success stories reveal that there are many ways to eliminate the usual risks of management consulting and to multiply its pay-offs. It is amazing that clients have permitted consultants to stick with the dismal conventional paradigm so tenaciously.

Why must mountains of information, data, insights, ideas, and innovations be amassed during a project, assembled in final reports, and then dumped onto the desks of client managers in doses beyond their capacity to absorb and use? There is no reason. Projects can be designed to yield recommendations that the client can respond to. Why should client managers have to assume full responsibility for translating the consultant's inputs into bottom-line results? There is no reason. The achievement of some meaningful result, as defined by the client, can be made the central focus of every consulting project. Highly leveraged consulting is not only a more valuable way to work, it is a more pleasant way to work. Clients and consultants enjoy working together to produce results.

In the chapters that follow, I will show how both clients and consultants can move toward results-focused high-impact consulting. You might want to think of a specific consulting project that you, either as a client or a consultant, are working on or plan to begin in the near future. Keep that project or potential project in mind as you read ahead so you will have a tangible, real-world situation against which to test the ideas in this book.

PART TWO

The Architecture of High-Impact Management Consulting

4

Define Goals in Terms of Client Results Instead of Consultant Products

I was invited to explore the possibility of assisting a rapidly growing food service company with an urgent problem. Its creditors had eased some tough demands, because the company had forecast breaking even in the coming year. After the first five months, however, sales were running well behind the company's projections.

Initial discussions quickly revealed one major step that could generate some progress immediately and possibly even ensure the company's survival: concentrate on increasing sales in the one major division that was the worst performer while encouraging the other divisions to continue the improvement steps they already had under way. There were many ideas among senior managers about how this could be done, but these ideas were not being acted on. Instead, the senior management group was spending much of its time on a number of developmental and planning activities led by a small internal consulting group.

Here are some of the activities that were being carried forward by the internal consulting group in the earnest belief that they were contributing to making the company more profitable:

First, they created a "timeless vision" for the company. They developed a set of corporate goals and carefully honed the wording (for example: "Profitability: To maximize the long-term value of the company" and a number of similar statements).

They created a set of corporate values ("Sustain our energy and commitment to the company mission while maintaining a healthy balance between personal and work life" and similar statements).

They developed a company strategy that included selling the company's product "not only through our own retail stores but through any channel (wholesale, retail, or mail order) that facilitates customer access to products."

They discussed and wrote out an expansion strategy.

They laid out a list of items under the heading "Strategic Focus" that began with "Our organizational excellence will become more and more important in the increasing competitive environment" and continued with a number of similar statements.

They created a one-year plan that began with "To *focus* our efforts on improving our business processes with a major focus on investing in people and with the goal of being profitable in the fiscal year" and continued with a number of similar statements.

They created a six-year vision, which began with "To be one of the top three companies" in their business in their part of the country "with the best business processes to support this," and continued with a number of similar statements.

They created a company planning process and a calendar of the key planning events for the coming year.

They launched a number of "process and planning" activities, each under the aegis of the CEO or another senior manager. These included developing a model for expansion; developing a prospecting telemarketing system; developing an on-line inventory system; developing a production forecasting system; developing a production planning and scheduling system; developing a plant process and equipment control system; developing an order entry and order scheduling system; developing an order fulfillment and inventory management system; developing a customer feedback process; and about fifteen or twenty more of these.

The consulting group thoroughly researched each of these projects and assessed them for their impact on customer satisfaction, their probability of success, their ease of implementation, and another half-dozen factors. The result was hundreds of rating scores on several pages of matrices.

Here was a business in difficulty, with some very urgent performance improvement requirements, but its management group was investing endless time in all these activities. The reason is that, to the internal consulting group, the key to attaining better results was to overcome the gaps and weaknesses in the organization's formal structures, systems, and processes.

The behavior of this internal consulting group illustrates the fallacy that guides most conventional consulting, internal or external. According to the conventional paradigm, if you want to produce better results, the first step is to build in all of the *presumed contributors* to better results; once you lay that groundwork, and do so properly, results will naturally follow.

When we explored with this company's management the possibility of focusing directly and immediately on achieving some performance improvements in the poorly performing division, a few of the senior managers favored the idea. But the concept created consternation among the CEO and the internal consultants. The idea of aiming directly at achieving some better results at once—the heart of the high-impact consulting paradigm—sounds as odd to most conventional consultants and their clients as the roundness of the earth sounded to Christopher Columbus's contemporaries.

Consider, for example, an automotive-parts plant whose customers were turning away from it because of quality and delivery problems:

To solve the plant's problems, a group of consultants helped management launch weekly employee-involvement team meetings focused on improving quality. After six months these teams had generated hundreds of suggestions and abundant goodwill among plant employees but no significant improvement in quality or delivery. It was a typical activities- rather than results-oriented effort.

When the division general manager introduced the plant's management to a results-oriented consultant, they agreed to try the consultant's approach on one production line. The manager of that line began by agreeing with his people that they would try to reduce by 30 percent the frequency of their most prevalent defect, and to do so within two months. This sharply focused goal was achieved, and the success created a model for an expanded, plantwide improvement process.

Both activity-centered strategies and results-driven strategies aim to strengthen performance. But as the experience of the food service company and the automotive parts plant show, the activities path is littered with the remains of endless preparatory investments that fail to yield the desired outcomes. The results-driven approach stakes out specific targets and then identifies the necessary resources, tools, and action plans to reach them.

Mistaking Means for Ends, Activities for Results

Activity-centered programs typically advance a managerial tool, technique, or direction. One reason for the rapid growth of consulting is that many managers believe that if they can only discover and carry out the right improvement *activities* it will inevitably lead to actual *improvements*. That is certainly what the food service company's managers believed. This perspective confuses ends with means and processes with outcomes. Consultants encourage this view by telling managers that they need not—in fact, should not—focus on improving results directly, because that approach is bound to be tactical and shortsighted. Once the fundamentals are in place, managers are told, the results will eventually take care of themselves.

But, in fact, activity-based consulting projects often have little or no impact on the client's bottom line. That should not be surprising, since the consultants in charge of such projects accept no responsibility beyond delivering a consulting product their client will accept. They do not place their reputation on the line and state that they will collaborate with the client to help deliver measurable improvements. And since the consulting product itself is what they are evaluated on, consultants operate on the idea that the more thoroughly their product is developed, the better. This leads to long cycle times as the consultant focuses on doing a thorough and correct job of research and analysis instead of helping the client take direct aim at achieving results.

Activity-centered programs continue to gain momentum in the business world, even though there is virtually no evidence to justify the massive investments companies make in them. Why are so many companies continuing to pour money and energy into these types of projects? They do it for the same reason that previous generations invested in zero-based budgeting, Theory Y, the Management Grid, quality circles, and the like. The daunting pace of change and exhausting competitiveness of business today make many managers willing to adopt approaches that appear sophisticated and sound plausible, even if they are not supported by any evidence.

Beginning with Results

In the high-impact consulting paradigm, clients and consultants take aim from the first moment at achieving some tangible results. Not programs. Not systems. Not reports. Not recommendations. Not studies with better answers. Not strategy formulations. None of these, unless they inherently include the delivery of some measurable bottom-line results. This means that if the *client's* goal is lower manufacturing costs, for example, then the *project's* goal will be to produce measurable cost savings. Whatever tools or methods the consultants might use, the focus will be on actually lowering the client's costs.

Let's see how this concept played out in the Department of Mental Health in Connecticut.

Like every other state, Connecticut has been plagued by rising workers' compensation costs from on-the-job employee injuries. In the Department of Mental Health, the most serious safety hazards for employees were the patients themselves. Lifting and transferring patients caused one category of problems. In addition, a small minority of violent patients caused many injuries. Employees were hurt. Morale suffered. Work was disrupted. And workers' compensation indemnity and medical care was increasingly costly to the state.

A number of "activities" steps had been carried out: safety training, research accidents, publicity to educate employees about the costs of accidents. And so on. Some of these programs were developed by state-employed staff consultants and some by outside consultants. The results were the same: the injury rate continued to increase, disrupting ward equanimity and patient care. The cost of disability compensation continued to accelerate.

FAIRFIELD HILLS: A RESULTS-FOCUSED EFFORT

As part of the state's Executive Management Program, a consultant from our firm was working with a group of managers that included the head nurse of the wards at Fairfield Hills, one of the state's mental health institutions. She thought that more training and additional staff might help solve the worker injury problem. Since there was no evidence that past training had had much impact and there was no budget for more people, the consultant suggested that perhaps they might try setting a specific goal for the reduction of worker injuries and then try to achieve it. While the suggestion seemed odd, since the head nurse felt that the goal had to be zero injuries, they agreed to try to reduce

the incidence of patient violence by 10 percent. This very modest goal reflected their lack of confidence that they could really
reduce worker injuries. They focused on two wards only, to make
sure the approach would work before involving other wards.
After some further discussion, a team was assembled under the
leadership of a nursing supervisor and given the task of achieving
the goal within three months on wards A and B.

Now for the first time there was some accountability for
results, shared by client and consultant. There was a measurable
goal. And, with some consulting assistance, the team began to
create a work plan, based not on some general principles of what
would be good to include in a safety program but on what would
be needed to reduce incidents that cause injury on those two
specific wards. They created new charts for tracking the nature
and time of patient incidents. They tested new ways to anticipate and avoid incidents. Nursing staff, aides, administrators,
and psychiatrists worked together as they had never done before.

During the three months of the experimental period, the
number of staff injuries dropped to two, compared to eight
during the same three months the previous year, and lost work
days were 11, compared to 144 the previous year.

By realizing these dramatic results, the hospital's management and the participants in the experiment moved from
being victims of a problem to being problem solvers. They
began to develop some confidence that they might be able to
manage an effective safety improvement process.

The head nurse at Fairfield Hills extended the process to all
six wards, and the injury rate from patient incidents actually
dropped by 85 percent and stayed there, year after year. Beyond
achieving these dramatic results at Fairfield Hills, the experiment proved to be the spark that ignited a statewide effort.

NORWICH HOSPITAL: BUILDING ON SUCCESS

In response to the urging of the state's workers' compensation
manager, Bob Finder, the superintendent of Norwich Hospital,

Garrell Mullaney, decided to test the results-focused approach to controlling the skyrocketing cost of workers' compensation. Norwich was a much larger facility than Fairfield Hills, and at the time it had one of the highest worker injury rates in the state. The work was sponsored by the Connecticut Quality of Work Life Committee, a state-sponsored union-management collaboration. Rather than tackle the problem all at once, Mullaney and consultants Suzanne Francis and Matthew McCreight agreed to focus at first on just two high-incidence wards from the hospital's more than twenty wards. He asked a team from each of these high-incidence wards to make significant measurable reductions in the number of staff injuries, and he made it clear that the role of the consultants was to help the teams do that. The hospital union supported and collaborated in the project.

The consultants helped the team members visualize how a results-focused experiment might work. Each team established some specific, ambitious goals. Both teams enjoyed considerable success in meeting those goals. The initial projects at Norwich reduced incidents of patient violence more than 60 percent from the previous year. That project, in 1988, was the beginning of a three-year program during which Mullaney expanded the program to all of Norwich, mobilizing more than twenty teams in the effort. Eight internal facilitators were trained to support the teams' work; the external consultants supported the internal facilitators and helped hospital management provide overall leadership and direction.

Meanwhile, other facilities began to participate. These used an even more leveraged approach, training their internal facilitators right from the start. The first four pilot wards at Connecticut Valley Hospital reduced safety-related incidents by 30 percent and lost work days by 70 percent compared to the previous year. At the same time, safety-related incidents *increased* by 10 percent in the hospital's other wards.

In 1990, the third year of the program, Norwich continued to expand its effort. Connecticut Valley added eight additional wards and support departments to its program. The out-side consultants' main role by that time was to train internal facilitators to support the work of an expanded number of teams. And Cedarcrest, another hospital, began its participation with three projects.

In 1993, the Quality of Work Life State Steering Committee asked my consulting firm to work with them to extend the safety improvement project statewide, not only in the Department of Mental Health but also in other departments. Consultants Suzanne Francis, Matthew McCreight, and Keith Michaelson worked with steering committee staff members Jane Fleishman and Chris Lassen, together with Paul Ashton of the Department of Mental Retardation, to implement the program throughout that department as well as in the Mental Health and the Public Health and Addiction Services Departments.

The head of each institution and the union representative chose two people to be trained as facilitators. These individuals in turn helped launch the teams at their own institution, with backup from the Quality of Work Life staff and the external consultants. The work was increasingly supported by internal staff members trained by the consultants to advance the process. In addition to building a large group of internal facilitators in the facilities of the three participating agencies, a few state-level people were developing the ability to spearhead an expanding statewide effort with very little outside consulting help.

In 1994, the Department of Mental Retardation's safety ombudsman, Paul Ashton, with help from Quality of Work Life staff, worked across the entire state in a number of the department's facilities and succeeded in reducing workers' compensation costs by $5 million a year, a 23 percent reduction. Ashton and the Quality of Work Life staff produced an additional $3 million a year in savings in workers' compensation the following year.

Thus, step by step, the project expanded through different state agencies, producing huge cumulative savings for the state. It was able to do so because each step along the way consisted of a results-focused project that produced measurable improvement.

Making measurable results the primary, immediate goal of a consulting project, as we did in Connecticut, is the first and most radical shift traditional consultants and their clients must make in adopting a high-impact, results-focused strategy. It is also the most critical, for the following reasons:

- Concentrating on a clear, short-term goal stimulates the performance-enhancing zest factors described earlier, because the client organization's own people are clearly accountable, with the consultant's help, for obtaining results.

- Because the client and consultant share the common goal of producing real results, they are motivated to work together. A partnership mode is encouraged, in contrast to the conventional approach of having the consultant do the studies and the client then attempt to produce the results.

- In a project with a sharp focus and clearly measurable outcomes, both client and consultant can ascertain what works and what does not.

- Finally, achieving a measurable success together is a joyous and reinforcing experience for both client and consultant. This is quite different from the typical conventional project, in which the consultant labors long and hard and then dumps a massive implementation task in the client's lap.

Translating Client Requirements into Results-Focused Projects

Making the shift to focusing on results is not difficult, but it is a major psychological wrench for most consultants (and many clients). Consultants frequently assert that results-focused projects are possible in only a very limited number of situations. We have found that it is possible to carve out results-oriented projects in response to virtually any client requirement.

Michael Hammer and James Champy, in their book *Reengineering the Corporation* and in numerous articles, have pointed out that many business processes evolved over time without being studied in a disciplined way.[1] Consequently, many are wasteful and inefficient. "Reengineering" and process redesign projects are aimed at remedying this situation. These techniques are focused on improving processes, however, rather than on achieving measurable results. Results can be designed into reengineering projects, however, as these examples show:

PROCESS MAPPING AND PROCESS REDESIGN

The order processing system at MVE, Inc., a company that manufactures cryogenic containers, was not working well. There were many problems and complaints. Instead of aiming at the broad goal of improving order processing, an initial project focused on reducing the error frequency in one category of orders through process improvement.

Manulife Insurance in Toronto was trying to reduce its turnaround time for issuing a certain category of new policies. Many activities had been launched to help achieve this goal, but they were not working. Seven different functions were involved in meeting the goal. One of the worst delays was caused by employees' placing problem applications in a "pending file." The first project was to "improve the processing of applications so that in six weeks we reduce the average number of applications in the pending file from 1,200 to under 1,000."[2]

COST REDUCTION

General Electric Lighting was not satisfied with the costs being incurred by breakage of fragile lamps. Traditionally manufacturing, the warehouse, and customer service had each worked on reducing breakage within their own bailiwick. As part of GE's "Workout" process (described in Chapter Eight), however, an interfunctional team was given the job of reducing breakage. With the help of a consultant, they decided that instead of doing an exhaustive study of breakage for hundreds of products and a dozen or more handling points, they would select one product and try to achieve some measurable reduction within sixty days.

They selected six-foot fluorescent tubes, a high-volume and relatively high-breakage product. Over several days a small subgroup traced the product from manufacturing to delivery and reported back to the full team. The team suggested using better (though slightly more costly) pallets and some space fillers in the trucks used to ship the product. Well before the sixty days had passed, the savings achieved were several million dollars a year. The expenses incurred were minor. Less than six consulting days were needed, and the dividends were already rolling in as the other product lines were attacked.

Rodney Blanckenberg, a South African consultant, helped managers at Hunt, Leuchars & Hepburn conduct a "hundred-day action project" to increase the number of eucalyptus logs the company could load onto a single railcar. Costs had to be reduced because the logs were for use as supports in gold mines, which were then suffering some economic hardship. Step one was a two-day workshop on the subject with all the company's managers involved in the process. With a total of about four or five consulting days from Blanckenberg plus some internal facilitation by a human resources officer, John Murray, the average load per car went from thirty-two tons to thirty-seven tons. This was followed by a similar project that achieved major savings in the costs of the labor and wire used in loading the cars. These projects launched thirteen years of continuing improvement at the company.

New Product Development

A division of Motorola wanted to reduce its fourteen- or fifteen-month cycle time for developing new products. Projects to improve long cycle times are almost always abstract and process-oriented. At the time, however, there were two specific (and important) new products that the division had promised to release many months before but had not yet been completed. A consultant helped them design a results-focused project to bring those two products successfully to market within ninety days, the newly promised date. In order to achieve this result, the consultant helped the client team test some new approaches, including parallel instead of sequential development steps and more disciplined management of all the elements of the project. When the team was able to achieve the targeted results, the methods were then tried on several other products and gradually institutionalized as part of the division's new product development process.

Improved Customer Service and Relationships

An office products company was having difficulty shifting its orientation from selling to small stationery and office supply outlets to the new superstores that were beginning to dominate the marketplace. They had many activities under way to facilitate the shift but had little to show for their effort. With the help of a consultant, they selected one important chain of superstores and set the goal of moving from an "acceptable supplier" rating to a "preferred supplier" rating within four months.

Backlog Reduction

At SmithKline Beecham, accelerated product development was placing a tremendous strain on the company's clinical data management unit. Each year the unit processes thousands of case report forms (CRFs) containing data from clinical trials at sites around the world. While some of their work had been contracted out, the group was faced with a backlog of eighty thousand CRFs, plus an accelerating flow of new ones. The group's management set a goal of reducing the backlog to ten thousand CRFs within four months. A consultant worked with fifty of the group's people to collect their ideas on how to achieve what looked like an almost impossible goal. They devised five major new ways to process the CRFs; each was advanced by a "champion" and some team members. Each team agreed on specific short-term deadlines. At the end of slightly more than three months, the number of CRFs had been reduced to fewer than ten thousand.

Even "soft" issues like management development and training can be done in a results-oriented way.

MANAGEMENT DEVELOPMENT AND TRAINING

American Greetings, the greeting card publishers, had to rapidly accelerate the development of its senior leadership people to head various expansion efforts. Consultant Harlow Cohen helped Harvey Levin, human resources senior vice president, and Mark Schantz, head of management development, carry out the following process. Four high-potential managers were identified. The person to whom each of them reported identified a few important performance improvements for the candidate to achieve in the very near future. One sales manager, for example, had to improve margins by more clearly differentiating between the more profitable products and the less profitable products and then taking appropriate steps to shift sales emphasis. Another had to reduce inventories. A third had to cut the new product development cycle. In each case, some short-term, measurable goal was specified, and it was made clear the managers were to provide leadership but not try to achieve the goals themselves. The external and internal consultants helped the managers organize the process to achieve their goals. They all succeeded, and beyond the bottom-line results, each candidate honed his skills in making things happen. They demonstrated what they were capable of achieving, and each was promoted shortly thereafter. All four of the participating managers now occupy high-level positions in the company, and the results-driven development process is being used with other high-potential managers.

Managers responsible for the creation or modification of large systems, and the consultants who support them, often aver that it is difficult if not impossible to design such a major project around achieving measurable results. Only after the system is implemented can specific goals be set, they say. The following case illustrates that this assertion may not be 100 percent valid.

LARGE-SCALE SYSTEMS INSTALLATIONS

In order to reduce inventory costs in the four commissaries that supply food to its passenger trains, the onboard services function of VIA Rail, Canada's national rail passenger service, decided to build an inventory control system. A consulting team of corporate systems people was assigned. In order to "involve the client," they created a steering committee of supervisors from one commissary.

The steering committee met monthly in the system group's "war room," surrounded by flowcharts, bubble charts, and other technical material. When the systems professionals made proposals about reporting formats, frequency of reporting, and data accumulation methods, committee members replied without demonstrating much grasp of the subject.

After about three or four months, the director of onboard services inquired about the group's progress. He was told that the project was moving ahead well and that the system would probably be ready for initial testing in about another year. Meanwhile, inventory costs were mounting. Impatient to produce some tangible improvement in the current year, the director challenged one of his commissaries to reduce inventory costs by $30,000 within three months. In this he was encouraged by Harvey Thomson, an associate of mine who was working with VIA at the time.

The head of this commissary put together a small team under the direction of a section head to accomplish this goal. The team was assisted by one of the corporate systems people and Thomson. The team focused on reducing inventory costs associated with one type of inventory (perishables). They identified some possible experimental steps and then put them to the test. The systems consultant developed some forms to help the team track and report data on this one class of inventory.

The team reduced the costs associated with perishable inventories by more than 75 percent in just over five weeks. With this success behind them, they went on to tackle other classes of inventory. Meanwhile, the director of onboard services extended the effort to the other three commissaries.

Within six months, VIA's annual inventory costs had been reduced by more than a quarter of a million dollars— many months before the overall system was even to be tested.

There were two other benefits realized by the shift to a results-focused approach. First, the systems consultant was able to use what he learned from the focused experiment with perishables to strengthen the design of the overall inventory control system. Second, the commissary supervisors who participated learned how to manage inventory levels in a planned, systematic fashion. This enabled them to be much better clients in the larger consulting project and much better users of the complete system when it was finally introduced.

This case illustrates that when internal consultants operate in the conventional mode, focusing all of their energy on developing professional products (in this case, a new inventory control system), they can become as estranged from the operating units of their organization as any conventional outside consultant. When they share with their clients a commitment to a bottom-line result, on the other hand, they almost automatically shift into the role of colleagues and allies. The ultimate result is a more successful change effort overall.

STRATEGIC PLANNING

Some years ago, Frank Green, then head of PPG Industries' Fiber Glass Products division, realized that a drastic shift in the nature of the fiberglass business was beginning to occur. After twenty-five years of growth as essentially a commodity business, the industry would in the future have to provide tailor-made products possessing a high degree of technical sophistication. This meant that the competitive advantage would no longer be with those companies that could manufacture an acceptable product at lowest cost but rather with those that could engineer products to meet each customer's unique requirements. Green eschewed the idea of cranking up a large-scale culture-change program. Instead, working with a results-focused consultant, he and his key associates selected one new product family for which they wanted more sales. They set this goal: they would develop three new "chopped-strand" products and be selling at least eight hundred thousand pounds per month of those products to six or more new customers within three years. This rather long-term goal was broken down into a series of subgoals. Thus, with this specific result targeted, the business had taken its first step into the new era.

These examples show how a focus on results can be introduced into almost any type of consulting project if there is determination to do it. Targeting a concrete result does not obviate the need for research, conceptual and strategic thinking, and many of the other traditional consulting activities; it just keeps everyone focused on some measurable end product.

Obstacles to a Focus on Results

Although the results-focused consulting project has many powerful advantages and is not all that difficult to implement, both consultants and client managers are often resistant to trying it. It is necessary, therefore, to pause and examine possible sources of resistance.

Consultant Roadblocks

First, why do consultants resist a results focus?

Fear of Losing Control. When consultants define a project in terms of the tasks they will perform and the products they will deliver, they are describing something that they know they will be able to do. The steps are clear to them, and nothing stands between them and certain "success." As soon as a bottom-line result is promised, the consultant's success depends on the client's behavior. This can be very uncomfortable for consultants.

Information Addiction. Consultants are often convinced that they cannot set any specific results goals until they do their research. "How do you know what is really possible until you do the study?" they ask. Or even worse, they maintain that, "If you set a goal at the beginning and it is not the right one, you might take the client down the wrong path."

Need for an Escape Hatch. Agreeing to do the technical, analytical part of a project and then letting the client take responsibility for achieving results is safe as well as logical. If for some reason a job doesn't work out, the consultant can explain that the project was great, but the client undermined it.

Some years ago, Professor Chris Argyris of Harvard demonstrated in crystal-clear terms how this is done. Here is his explanation of the client's termination of a project that he was conducting with the senior management of the *New York Times* (disguised as the *Daily Planet* in Argyris's book): "The fact that the client did not choose to continue beyond these learning experiences is a sign of their own failure, not failure of the intervention process. What we are left with is strong evidence that when forty top members of the *Daily Planet* had an opportunity to make their organization one that learns and examines itself, they retreated from the challenge."[3] Many consultants would readily share this sort of conclusion privately with other consultants, but very few have had the chutzpah to announce it publicly.

Consultants' explanations have not changed much in the intervening twenty years. Here is James Champy explaining shortfalls in reengineering efforts: "The obstacle is management."[4]

The Profit Motive. Endless activities and preparations are profitable to consultants. Many popular business fads have become core activities for consulting firm practice. In a 1994 article the *Wall Street Journal* took aim at one of the great many consultant-driven fads, the formulation of company "vision statements": "Facing tougher competition and tighter budgets more companies, cities, schools and even individuals are taking stock of who they are, what they do and how they plan to do it better. The result: a proliferation of 'missions,' 'visions,' 'values,' and the like, emblazoned on annual reports, factory walls, and—companies hope—the psyches of their workers."[5] The article went on to describe the key roles played by consultants in helping companies spend time and energy on this activity.

Client Roadblocks

Clients also play a significant role in perpetuating activities-focused consulting rather than results-driven projects.

Risk Avoidance. When a senior manager hires a consultant to do a typical activities-focused project, he takes a very modest risk. If the project works out, he can claim credit for it. If there are no results, he can blame the consultant's work.

Sticking in the Mode. Most senior managers who supervise internal consultants or engage consulting firms are so used to the conventional consulting paradigm that they don't even question it. They don't expect consultants to commit to more than doing the consulting work and carrying out their programs. They have never seen consultants work as partners with clients in a results-oriented mode, and thus have no mental model of how it ought to work.

This stereotypical way of viewing consulting input can cause considerable grief for internal consulting groups and the organizations in which they operate. What often happens is that senior managers who face a problem decide that an internal group holds the key to success. So they promulgate the consultant's expertise or methodology as a kind of magic cure. In Connecticut's mental hospitals, for example, before they really learned how to reduce worker injuries, you can be sure that they mandated certain safety training courses as "the cure." In other organizations, the desire by senior management to improve quality is the fuel that drives their internal staff consulting groups to create corporate quality training, quality procedures, quality inspections, and quality contests, without any necessary connection to quality results. In the same way, the desire to increase productivity in many organizations translates into pressure on human resource staff groups to reconstruct their compensation systems to provide incentives for productivity.

In this way, major portions of the time and energy of a great many internal staff consulting groups are invested in activities that have right-sounding names (such as "Profit Improvement Process" or "Becoming a Total Quality Company") and are definitely intended to lead to results—but have no demonstrable connection to such results. Often, frustrated by the lack of progress achieved by these programs, senior managers will encourage their internal staff consultants to augment their efforts with some external consulting, as if simply increasing the level of activity will increase the likelihood of achieving tangible results.

Reassurance. There is something reassuring to impatient managers about having seemingly competent, confident consultants bustling about their organization. As these consultants go about their work, they cite previous successes, spotlight weaknesses the managers have been concerned about, and install tools and methods that appear to be better than the ones they replaced. Occasionally their work even seems to lead to some significant bottom-line improvements. All of these can provide some psychological comfort when managers have reached the limit of what they know how to do but the results are still not good enough. There is a sense of purpose, of directed action, of high-level professionalism. And if the consultants doing the work come from a well-known firm, so much the better.

Demand Results!

Managers, it is time to liberate yourselves. Only when your consultants agree to help you produce some measurable results have they really cast their lot with you. That is the moment when they abandon the consultant's traditional safety net, the rationalization that "We gave them a good system, but they just weren't able to get the results."

When consultants actually share a commitment to achieving measurable results, to lowering costs or improving quality, they will exert more effort to find ways to use the skills and talents that already exist within the organization. They will concentrate on finding the shortest path to results and working toward the outcomes that are easiest to produce.

Thomas Kivlehan, vice president of reengineering for the publisher Simon & Schuster, reported that several "big six" consulting firms agreed to bid on a project for him in which their fee would be keyed to the achievement of some measurable result. When asked whether there was any difference between their approach to that project and their more usual approach, Kivlehan responded: "There was a big difference. They were much more insistent about demanding participation by key individuals from our company. And all of a sudden they were spelling out requirements that we had to meet in conducting the project. They wanted assurance they could meet with the executive committee to resolve issues. They wanted a certain amount of executive committee involvement in the project and support for it. Consultants basically don't pay any attention to these issues when they are doing one of their regular jobs."

As Kivlehan's quote makes very clear, focusing a consulting project on specific, measurable results produces a very healthy shift in the behavior of both the consultant and the client. They join forces to produce a measurable bottom-line result. At the end of a project, both share a sense of accomplishment that is vastly different from the reaction to simply having installed a new system or changed a method. They have both learned about what the other party can contribute and how to best pool their knowledge. And they have created momentum that can open the way to more ambitious progress.

5

Match Project Scope to What the Client Is Ready to Do

I sometimes pose the following question to groups of consultants: "Assume you are going into a gambling casino, and you have this choice—you can walk directly to the roulette wheel and start betting your chips at once, or you can walk over to a reference manual that will tell you fairly reliably how the numbers will come up on the wheel. Which would you do?" This question is always rejected as too ridiculous for serious consideration.

Then I point out that most consultants chose the "ridiculous" first option over the second one practically every day of their life. Most consultants will thoroughly explore the technical and operational issues related to a new assignment, but they will fail to investigate the client's willingness and ability to actually implement the recommendations the project might produce.

The publisher of a large metropolitan newspaper invited a consulting firm to do a study on how the paper could reduce costs. "With the cost of newsprint rising and competition for the advertiser's dollar getting tougher every day," the publisher told the consultants, "I need to cut costs significantly. And I don't mean nickels and dimes." The consultants proposed a study design, and the publisher accepted it. He encouraged the consultants to study anything they thought might be relevant.

The consulting team was able to identify major opportunities for cost reductions in nearly every part of the organization. It was a diamond mine of opportunity for cost reduction. Non-value-added work was being performed in nearly every function. Work that flowed from department to department was poorly coordinated, and when errors occurred, the main preoccupation was with shifting blame rather than making corrections. The reporting and editing staff felt that reducing costs and boosting efficiency were not subjects they should be concerned with.

The consultant team gathered it all in and then assembled a report outlining the major opportunities and suggesting a comprehensive plan to achieve significant improvements. They looked forward to the possibility of a great deal of exciting and productive work helping make it all happen. The publisher met with them alone to hear their report. "I want to get a sense of it first before I drop it on my people," he told them. He spent several hours with the consultants and listened to their report thoughtfully. He asked many questions, but he did not make any commitments to take action. "This is pretty fundamental stuff," he said. "I need to think about it."

A few weeks later, when the consultants called, as agreed, to set a time to plan the next steps, the publisher put the meeting off for a while. And then he put it off for a few more weeks. And he did it again. And again. Finally the consultants realized there would be no big assignment for them. Nor any big cost reductions for the paper.

To see this senior executive turn his back on so many millions of dollars in annual savings that were within such easy reach rankled them. They spoke disparagingly about the publisher's "lack of guts," and then they turned their attention to the next client.

Since the newspaper publisher seemed so interested in reducing costs, the consultants assumed that when they suggested a plan for reducing costs, he would do what was necessary to implement it. So they examined staff size, reporter deployment, use of news services, information systems, accounting and control systems, office operations, newsprint purchasing, and printing and distribution procedures.

The consultants did not, however, attempt to investigate the lengths to which the publisher might actually be willing to go to effect their recommended improvements. The consultants did not find out whether he had discussed the need for cost reduction with his associates and, if so, whether they had understood and supported his decision to reduce costs significantly. They did not find out whether the publisher had ever launched and sustained an effort to effect significant change within the organization. They did not find out how willing he might be to tangle with his associates if they all insisted that the consultants' ideas were unsound. In short, the consulting team walked in and threw all their chips on the table for one big bet, without first digging into the "manual"—the evidence in the client environment—that contained the clues about what might work and what would be unlikely to work in that situation.

As the newspaper example illustrates, such gambles often fail. Moreover, consultants rarely seek to discover *why* such a failure occurred. They may ascribe it to the client's lack of motivation, lack of real interest in obtaining better results, and so forth. As the consultants see it, they have provided the "right" answers or solutions, and if the client fails to capitalize on them, there must be something wrong with the client.

Interestingly, clients are all too willing to accept the blame. Perhaps because consultants almost always deliver the products they promise to deliver, and because they usually deliver it in impressive formats, it is rare for clients to come right out and blame the consultants when a project's results are disappointing. In fact, it is not unusual to hear a client manager say about a consulting project that didn't accomplish much, "There were some very good ideas in that report. Too bad none of our people really wanted to do anything with it," or, "Too bad the marketing people didn't buy it." Or client managers reassure themselves, as the newspaper publisher may have done, that they have not really discarded the consultant's recommendations but have merely delayed implementing them.

Whether the client blames the consultant or the consultant blames the client or they both pretend a failure didn't occur, a consulting effort that doesn't yield results is a terrible waste. Whenever bright and able consultants come together with managers who want to effect improvement, but no real progress is achieved, a tragedy has occurred.

It is my firm conviction that virtually every consulting assignment could be successful if consultants, with the help of their clients, would develop the equivalent of the hypothetical casino reference manual. I refer to the process of creating this manual as "assessing client readiness." That means finding out while designing a project what the client is and is not likely to be willing or able to do when the time comes for decision and action. With this information in hand, the client and consultant can design the project to match what the client probably will be ready and able to do. The rest of this chapter describes how such a manual can be developed to enable clients and consultants to pursue a "sure win" approach to consulting.

Assessing Readiness in the Closet Case

The reader will recall from Chapter One the story of a magnificent consultant-installed closet system that went for naught when the family failed to maintain it. I have found that a good way to illustrate the concept of client readiness in seminars I teach is to try to identify the readiness factors in that case. After discussing the case with a group of consultants, I challenge them to think of questions that the closet consultants should have asked before they got started in order to be certain the project would be successful. Within six or seven minutes, a typical group of management consultants generally think of forty, fifty, or more questions that the closet consultants might have asked. See if you can think of eight or ten questions you would have asked before redesigning the closet. Then compare your questions with those suggested by other consultants (see Exhibit 5.1).

The exhibit contains only a small sampling of the kinds of questions that need to be asked to avoid failure but that consultants rarely

EXHIBIT 5.1. Readiness Questions in the Closet Case.

Factual Issues
- What exactly do you keep in the closet?
- Who uses it?
- How many times do you go into your closet each day?
- Do you change the contents each season, or is it the same year round?
- When was the last time you sorted through the closet and tossed out any unused articles?
- Are there other closets in the house, and what do you use them for?
- What's your ideal sorting system?
- What kind of shelving, lighting, or floor covering would you like in the closet?
- How quickly do you need this job completed?
- What do you think about the closet we redesigned for your friend?

Psychological Issues
- Why do you want to redesign your closet?
- What do you think doesn't work about the closet? What does?
- Do each of the people using the closet agree on what needs to be done—and how to do it?
- Does everyone in the family feel equally strong about the goal of closet redesign?
- Have you ever attempted to make improvements like this before? What was the outcome?
- How willing do you think the people who use this closet will be to change their habits, especially if they're in a hurry, to maintain a new setup?
- What do you envision will be different in your life after you redesign your closest?
- What behavior do think you'll need to change after the new closet is finished?

Defining the Project Goals
- What are you really hoping to accomplish from our work?
- Describe how things would be different were this project to be successful

EXHIBIT 5.1. *(continued)*

- Do you plan on using the closet for the same purposes after you redesign it?
- Do you want the new design of the closet to reflect utility, aesthetics, or both?
- How involved would you like to be in this project?
- What role or roles would you like us to play?

ask. If even some of the information suggested by the questions had been elicited, the closet consultants might have realized that the fully redesigned closet project would be a failure. Then they might have tried to conceive and suggest a more limited, "get-started" project.

When I ask consultants to suggest some possibilities for such get-started projects, inventive answers come rapidly. "Why not start by helping the family to get rid of stuff they don't use any more?" "How about seasonality? See if they can remove and store all the items not needed in the current season." "How about starting with just one category? Shoes, for example. Provide a way to store them. Then come back a few weeks later and see how that's working out."

Thus consultants who, in their own practice, may totally ignore readiness issues can devise many possible readiness questions for the closet consultant case. They can also quickly devise a dozen get-started projects to match the client readiness they discover.

If the newspaper's consulting team had used this very same approach with the publisher, their project could easily have been a success instead of a failure. Some simple questions would have revealed that the company had never carried out any major improvement projects. The publisher was an intellectual leader with a brilliant grasp of good journalism and deep convictions in his editorial stance. But he had never had to deal with any major conflicts within the organization. He had never had the experience of cutting people's budgets or requiring them to achieve new goals or make major improvements. It should have been clear to the consultants that a large-scale project was doomed to fail.

With this knowledge in mind, they might have suggested a few get-started projects designed to avoid too much controversy. Reduce overtime in a few departments, for example. Eliminate newsprint waste caused by mishandling the rolls. Reduce the frequency of typographical errors that require rework. With a menu of such possible projects, they could have explored with the publisher which he thought he could make happen successfully.

But wait. How could the consultant suggest such modest projects when the publisher had clearly said he was not interested in just cutting "nickels and dimes"? Consultants need to remember that by the time managers call for consulting help, they may be frustrated and irritated. Their comments may reflect these feelings. No matter how dramatically and impatiently managers declaim their wishes, however, consultants should not be panicked into taking self-defeating action. Even if the client hopes for the largest-scale changes imaginable, there is nothing inconsistent with suggesting some get-started projects to create momentum and test the waters. Doing so imposes no limits on how fast it can go from there.

How to Assess Readiness

This section presents some guidelines on how to assess readiness and take the gamble out of consulting projects. The first step is for both client and consultant to make a commitment to designing their project in terms of assessed readiness.

If you are a client, you should insist that any consulting project begin with some thoughtful speculation concerning possible project outcomes and what might be required of you and your people to make the project succeed. Then ask yourself whether you and your consultants are confident you will be able to do it. If you are uncertain about your answer, then you need to redesign the project until you can be more certain of the match between what will be required and what you will want to do and be able to do.

If you are a consultant, you need to experiment with including readiness testing in your exploratory discussions. This is not just a matter of proceeding through a long checklist (like the one in Exhibit 5.2) but of developing sensitivity to the issues. As with so many of the concepts in high-impact consulting, most experienced consultants already possess many of the skills needed to assess readiness. You need to try it out on your next project, and the one after that. You will easily develop more skills as you practice.

EXHIBIT 5.2. Readiness Assessment Checklist.

---

1. **Overall Motivation and Drive**
   - What is the client's motivation for this project? Is the client enthusiastic? passive? resistant? Does motivation seem to be different in different groups within the client organization?
   - What is the client's view of possible project gains?
   - Who wants change to take place? Who doesn't care? Who is against change?
   - To what extent does the project respond to a goal everyone says is important but on which they seem reluctant to work?
   - Are there other motivation issues?
2. **Resource Allocation and Commitment Level**
   - What is the client's view of the time, energy, and support that will be required to carry out the project?
   - Does the client expect to participate in the work? Is the client ready to do his or her part?
   - If other groups' or people's commitment is required, has it been (or is it being) secured?
   - Is it clear what the budget will be? Does the client's view of an appropriate budget match the consultant's?
   - Are there other resource issues?
3. **Climate for Change**
   - What kinds of pressures for change exist in the client organization? Where do they come from?
   - Where does the particular issue the consultant is focusing on fit into the client's hierarchy of concerns? Is it a top-priority issue or just something they feel they need to deal with?
   - Will the organization's climate support the kinds of changes the project might require?
   - Are there other climate issues?

EXHIBIT 5.2. (*continued*)

4. **Client's Technical Capacity and Change Management Skills**
   - What is the client's capacity to implement innovations and change? What do recent experiences suggest about whether the client will be able to carry out the changes and adaptations that the project might require?
   - What is the client's demonstrated capacity to absorb new ideas and exploit them usefully?
   - What is the client's experience with and knowledge about the particular issue the project is focusing on?
   - Are there other knowledge and skill issues?

5. **Client's View of the Consultants**
   - Has the client had some recent experience with this consulting group or with a similar group? How did that work out?
   - How does the client feel about these experiences? What can be learned from previous experiences that will strengthen the design of this project?
   - What is the client's overall attitude toward the consultants who will be working on the upcoming project?
   - Are there other client-consultant relationship issues?

6. **Client Understanding of the Project**
   - Has the client sharply defined project outcomes for himself or herself? What will be the client's measure of success?
   - Does the client understand the implications of the project for the organization?
   - What is to be the specific output or product of the project? Who is going to use it, and how? Is this understood in the same way by all key players?
   - Are there other client understanding issues?

7. **Scope and Pace of Project**
   - What is the client's "project attention span?" How quickly must the client see some tangible results? What kind of results?
   - What is the client's view of the appropriate scope and pace of the project? How big a project seems right to the client? What sort of pace does the client wish to pursue?
   - Are there other pace and scope issues?

8. **Other Success Factors**
   - Are there certain solutions that will be taboo or unacceptable in the client organization?

EXHIBIT 5.2. (*continued*)

- Do the client and consultant mean essentially the same thing in their use of key words describing the project?
- Are there other issues not yet addressed?

9. **Historical Perspective**
  - How did the current need evolve, and how long has the client been aware of the need?
  - How has the client attempted to deal with the issues until now? What has worked? What has failed to work?
  - How did the idea of using consulting assistance arise?

Exhibit 5.2 provides a systematic checklist of suggested readiness questions. It is written as though it is addressed solely to consultants, but clients also need to ask these questions of themselves. There may be some readiness issues in your own practice (if you are a consultant) or organization (if you are a manager) that are unique to your situation. Think about possible additional factors not on the list that might be relevant in your situation. One way to create your own personal readiness checklist is to think back on consulting projects that were disappointing to you (either as a client or as a consultant) and ask, "What kinds of information did we discover only after the project was under way or completed that we should have found out about before we began?"

Getting Comfortable with Assessing Readiness

One obstacle to good readiness assessment is the fact that in the initial, exploratory stages of a project, both the mangers considering hiring a consultant and the consultants they are interviewing want to look good to the other party and to their own associates. The desire to not be seen as incompetent or unknowledgeable may lead some participants, often unconsciously, to keep their doubts and uncertainties covered up. This tendency is definitely an obstacle to accurate readiness assessment. Both parties have to work diligently to make each other increasingly comfortable sharing realities instead of trying to project desirable images.

A consultant who wants to sharpen his or her readiness assessment skills should experiment with a few selected readiness questions. Until the process becomes second nature, consultants should prepare an inventory of possible questions before client meetings. The questions below provide some illustrations of how the subjects listed in Exhibit 5.2 can be addressed with clients.

- Describe your view of how things will be different if this project is successful.
- Why have you decided to get this project started at this particular moment?
- What are some of the other major challenges you are facing in your job? How does this project relate to them?
- Who will have to participate in this project? Do they share your views of the situation?
- Have your people worked with consultants before? How did it work out?
- Do you have any thoughts on how your people and the consulting team should work together?
- Have you ever carried out any projects like this one? How did they work out?

Notice that the questions all call for elaboration rather than a simple yes or no answer. As consultants gain experience probing into readiness issues, they develop more skill in selecting the right questions.

The "What If?" Test

Another useful way to test client readiness is for client and consultant simply to ask "What if . . . ?" By describing a project's possible outcomes at the outset, the client and the consultant can have a healthy dialogue on its potential value. This avoids the risk that the client will say, "Oh, this isn't what we were expecting" when the project is completed. The "What if?" scenario is one additional way to avoid nasty surprises.

One division of a large corporation in the chemicals, plastics, and glass business was interested in the possibility of achieving forward integration through an acquisition. First they needed to identify likely acquisition candidates. The division hired a large, well-known consulting firm that had done considerable work for it in the past and asked the firm to conduct a study to forecast future industry trends and predict the likely winners and losers.

The study's primary finding was that within each of the industry segments being considered, the top one or two firms had excellent prospects while the others had much less promising futures. The dilemma was that the price-to-earnings multiples for the top one or two firms in each segment were unacceptably high. So, although the consultants made some specific acquisition recommendations, no action was taken.

This outcome was virtually inevitable from the outset. Almost all of the key players in the company would have been able, with the information they already possessed, to identify the same acquisition candidates—and they would have known that the cost of acquiring was far too high. The only way this project might have succeeded would have been if the consultant had found a relatively unknown company that could be purchased for a reasonable price. But there were very few companies in the segments studied, and all were already known to the client, anyway.

A "What if?" readiness assessment at the start could have saved this business time, money, and embarrassment. In such a scenario the consultants sketch the possible outcomes of their study before they take the first step. These are shared informally with a group of client people, and together the clients and consultants examine what it would take to act on the imagined recommendations. Would the possible benefits be worth the costs? What kind of resistance might be encountered? In the acquisition case, the price of the desirable companies would have surfaced in the very first discussion. The study that was done would never have been done. Perhaps some more constructive directions might have been pursued.

Another way to conduct a "What if?" readiness assessment is for the consultant to simulate, for discussion with the client, the products of the project. If one of the outcomes is to be a work flow, for example, the consultant can mock up a hypothetical model of what the process might look like after the project is complete and ask, "Would this help you get better results? How might it be made more useful?"

Hidden Verve

It would be a mistake to think of readiness testing solely as a method for limiting the scope of a project. As described in Chapter Three, organizations often possess considerable unexploited capabilities, and readiness testing can sometimes reveal them. Here is an example of how readiness testing mobilized the client to undertake an exciting project that had not been visualized previously:

In 1990 Motorola's Components Division was challenged to become a profitable business. This was a change from its previous role as a "strategic supplier" to other Motorola divisions. This shift required the division to make a 30 percent improvement in its bottom line. In working to achieve the goal, the division made many improvements in its cost structure, its product lines, its marketing and sales methods, and its manufacturing processes. Nevertheless, improvements in profits came very slowly. My firm was working with Motorola at the time, and Jerry Bruning, the division's general manager, invited us to help. He told us that the present plan called for arriving at break-even in twenty-four months, but that was much too far in the future. The process had to be accelerated. After several discussions, Bruning suggested we meet with his top team of about fourteen people to get their views.

At the meeting, after some preliminary introductions, my colleague Bob Neiman turned to the group and said, "We understand there is a two-year schedule for your division to become profitable. Further, we understand that there isn't even clear agreement on how that can be accomplished. I'd like to ask all of you to put yourself in the place of your general manager. If you were he, when would you insist that the division must break even? Write down the number of months you would allow, fold your paper, and pass it in. Do not sign your name."

A scale was drawn on the board, and as each paper was unfolded, Neiman marked the number. The lowest number was four months. The highest was eighteen months, a full half a year ahead of the budgeted time. The rest ranged in between.

This demonstration had a powerful effect on the group's motivation. Instead of the general manager or consultant having to convince them to move up the target date, here were their own estimates saying it was possible to accelerate the schedule. And sure enough, an acceleration plan was devised within the framework they had provided, and break-even was reached in less than a year.

On hearing that story, cynics sometimes ask, "But what if they had estimated that it would take much longer than twenty-four months?" Well, that too would have been important to know. Jerry Bruning, the general manager, would be no worse off, and he would at least be aware that there was no basis for his confidence that the pace could be accelerated. The priority for the consulting project in that case would have been to experiment with some very short-range action steps that might create momentum and open the minds of the group to the possibility of accelerating.

In this case, a successful acceleration strategy needed to start from the base of what the key players thought was possible. To believe that a consultant can do a study and then "prove" to the members of an organization that they can do better than they believe they can do is pure fantasy.

Bringing Readiness into Focus

Sometimes it is necessary not only to diagnose readiness, but to take steps to influence the level of readiness of the people who will be working with the consultant. This is a task for senior management and the consultant. Here is an example of how this played out in a specialty glass manufacturing facility (whose name is disguised), from the diary of Harlow Cohen, the consultant who led the work.

When we first started working with Vitrine Products, one of the first projects was to improve the efficiency of the 712 jet-air furnace which provided the molten glass for the bulk of the company's products. The furnace had performed at well below industry standards for the previous five years, and a variety of managerial efforts had failed to raise its efficiency.

Joe McCray, the vice president of manufacturing, and Ted Stevens, the plant manager, knew that every point of efficiency would contribute significant sums directly to the bottom line, not to mention the added throughput such gains might create.

When I met with Hank Granowski, the furnace superintendent, it quickly became clear that Hank was not ready to work with anyone to improve furnace efficiency, least of all a consultant who had no prior experience in the glass industry. He explained that he already had commissioned a technical team, headed by himself, to study the problem. They had been at work for the last four months, and he felt they had the situation well in hand even though no results could be demonstrated yet. He also believed that unless heavy capital expenditures were made to improve the furnace, progress would be minimal. Just one of the new systems he was proposing would have cost more than a million dollars.

He explained also that the scheduling of products to be run through the furnace was very poorly done and was a big contributor to furnace disruptions and inefficiencies.

McCray would not back away from the need to improve the furnace efficiencies and to do so without further capital investment. Plant manager Stevens drafted a fairly strong project assignment to Hank, stressing the importance of showing measurable results and doing so fairly soon. This was followed by a second strongly worded memorandum by vice president McCray.

After these memoranda, Hank agreed to meet with me again to develop a strategy. We decided that I would interview a number of the supervisors, process engineers, and hourly workers on the furnace to get their thoughts about possible improvement ideas. I talked to them and then summarized their suggestions in a work session with Hank and his furnace team. We also agreed, in order to avoid overlap with Hanks's technical team that had been at work for some months, that this project would focus only on operational improvements. And we were able to get the plant manager to freeze the "disruptive scheduling" during a one-week experimental period.

Hank was reluctant to set a goal more ambitious than raising efficiency by 2 percent. I argued that with a frozen schedule it should be possible to gain more. After further discussion, Hank agreed to set a goal of a 7 percent improvement. That was a very daring step since he had no experience to indicate that it could be done, but there were three factors that enabled Hank to venture: first, the agreement by the plant manager to freeze the schedule; second, the fact that we were going to provide some hands-on consulting help; and third, the fact that his commitment to the goal was only for the one experimental week.

Once Hank had agreed, we met with his people and went over the project ideas with them. They agreed to shoot for the seven-point increase, but only after it was pointed out that they were committing themselves for only the one-week experiment. Next we secured their ideas for improvement, and decided to concentrate on those that had the highest potential payoff and were easiest to implement.

Six project teams were organized, each with one specific area of responsibility, and we worked with those teams. By the time the experimental week came, just three weeks after the start of the project, furnace efficiency had improved 8 percent, four times Hank's original target. And it remained high after the experimental week. The paradox was that two weeks later, the scheduling went right back to the same old patterns (which, as Hank had correctly pointed out, was somewhat disruptive), but performance continued at the high levels reached during the experiment. It never dropped below that peak level until eighteen months later, when it was time to rebuild the furnace due to its age and deterioration.

Vitrine's vice president of manufacturing and the plant manager both supported this consulting project, but when the consultant put his toes in the water he saw that there was no match between the project goal and the readiness of the client who would have to achieve that goal. Even if Cohen had been the world's greatest expert on furnaces, his failure would have been guaranteed had he not moved deliberately to build the readiness of all participants and to avoid setting any goals that they would not accept as their own.

Mapping: Casting Light into the Shadows

When we see the hero in a Hollywood thriller walk into a darkened room, we anticipate that some shadowy figure will leap out and attack him. So it is in consulting projects, too. Wherever there are dark corners, a threatening figure may emerge from the shadows to announce that there is no budget for the project or the consultant's recommendations are simply unworkable.

The idea behind readiness testing is to gather information that will permit clients and consultants to design projects that eliminate, as much as possible, the likelihood of nasty surprises. One element of information that helps achieve this goal is the identification of all the people whose approval or cooperation will be essential for success. To avoid nasty surprises, the client and consultant need to shed light into all the dark corners where these figures may be lurking and identify them and the roles they might play. The process for accomplishing this is known as *client system mapping*. Its aim is to develop a clear *Who's Who* that identifies all the key players and influencers.

Mapping can be done by the consultant team, by the client team, or, preferably, by both working together. Step 1 in client mapping is to identify the full cast of characters, not merely the managers who are talking with the consultant. Exhibit 5.3 offers a checklist to help identify both the obvious and the less obvious players.

Step two is drawing the map. Once the cast of characters is identified, it is useful to sketch a diagram that portrays the place of

---

EXHIBIT 5.3. A Project's "Cast of Characters."

1. The client—the one person (or a clearly designated small group) with the principal accountability for achieving the targeted results, with the support of the consultant.
2. People who are active participants in the planning and implementation of the project.
3. Contributors to the project who are not involved directly in the work.
4. People whose job or job environment will be affected by project results: obvious winners and possible losers.
5. Project user groups and their representatives—such as a steering committee, a project review panel, and so on.
6. Senior managers, whose general support and positive views can have subtle but crucial impact.
7. The ultimate decision makers and budgetary authorities.
8. (Add your own categories . . .)

each of the key players and the relationships among them. This should be a dynamic portrayal that best conveys the client's and consultant's views of the dynamics among these people—it should not be a conventional organization chart. It should make it possible for the client and consultant to discuss readiness and relationship issues with greater clarity.

Some teams use various symbols to help sharpen the map, drawing a circle around people who are crucial to the project but have not been sufficiently involved in its planning, for example, or a check mark next to people who may oppose elements of the project or its conclusions.

Loading for Success

The most expensive way to learn about a mismatch between a project's design and the client's readiness is to carry out the project and then, after the time, money, and effort have been invested, discover that there is no way to move from the consultant's recommendations to the client's desired results.

Readiness testing, "What if?" scenarios, and client mapping can prevent this outcome. These steps take much of the gamble out of consulting work. When consultants and clients have carefully assessed all of the readiness issues that might be relevant to a project they are about to launch, they are able to load their project for success. They do this by carefully designing the project so that its goals are clearly achievable by the people who have to achieve them, even if they do have to stretch their capabilities somewhat.

Readiness exploration is an ongoing process, not a one-time event. After a project has begun, if any doubts arise about the match between the project design and the client's readiness to go forward, client and consultant share responsibility for insisting that the issue be addressed and the project design modified if necessary.

Consultants and clients who are considering long-term, ambitious, complex projects, such as totally reengineering a company's operations or replacing a series of outdated information systems with one massive new system, point out that it is virtually impossible to assess readiness accurately in such cases. They assert that the project's completion is so far off that it is impossible to predict the consultant's recommendations at the beginning. But that view of an assignment can easily be the first step toward a massive failure. Rather than abandoning the step of assessing readiness, a more logical choice in such cases might be to carve off a first-step subproject that can be completed quickly and can serve as a stepping-stone toward larger goals. The next chapter describes that strategy.

6

Aim for Rapid-Cycle Successes to Generate Momentum

Avionic Instruments designs and manufactures electronic control equipment for aircraft. For several years everybody in the company had been running faster and faster to keep up with the rapidly expanding demand for its products. Already breathless, senior management suddenly realized that demand was accelerating in 1996 at an even more radical pace. To respond would require major improvements in production planning, manufacturing processes, purchasing, inventory management, and quality control. At the same time, the company also needed to upgrade the skills of its entire workforce.

To help with this somewhat overwhelming situation, a traditional consultant would undoubtedly have begun with a comprehensive study of the company's operations (or perhaps several studies) and then . . . but you already know the rest.

In fact, consultants Keith Michaelson and Rich Heinich, working in a high-impact mode, saw that it would be easy to overload this already stretched-out company. He asked the company's managers whether there was any one product that was more critical than the others. There was such a product, so Michaelson helped them organize a cross-functional team

87

to expand its rate of production. The team set a goal: to double output within two months.

The team worked on ensuring parts availability, coordinating the scheduling of subassembly production with final assembly, and identifying and overcoming production bottlenecks. Within two months, they were able to double production. They set a similar goal for the next two months, and sure enough, they doubled production again.

Obviously, they had achieved dramatic success with this sharply focused project. More importantly, they developed considerable insight into how to manage expansion of the company's overall output.

The aim of conventional consulting is to formulate an overall solution and to share that vision with the client. This all-or-nothing approach on the part of the consultant almost inevitably leads to large-scale, long-term project designs. In this case it undoubtedly would have.

In high-impact consulting, rather than design an overall solution at once, the aim is to carve off a series of rapid-cycle attacks. One purpose for this is to create some measurable results for the client in the shortest possible time. The reinforcement of success, plus the knowledge gained by both client and consultant, creates the foundation for accelerated progress. The cumulative gains of a series of incremental improvements is actually as great as (or greater than) what large projects promise they will achieve "someday."

Many conventional consultants assert that shooting for rapid results should generally be avoided. They aver that taking action before carrying out a big study may cause the client to focus on tactics instead of strategy, improve a system that should be eliminated, or head south when they should be heading north.

I have used rapid-payoff projects as steps in large-scale client change projects in many dozens of organizations for over thirty years, and I have never seen a single example of these tragic outcomes. Nor have any of the other consultants who work in parallel modes. First, designing the initial project is a thoughtful process, not simply plucking a goal out of thin air. Second, initial projects can usually be carried out rapidly and for relatively little cost. In half the time it takes for just a study and analysis of a big blockbuster project, an initial rapid-cycle project will likely be over and done with and have paid for itself. Moreover, until the client and consultant have shared some successful experience in a number of modest projects, any attempt to carry out a complex, long-term change is basically just a Las Vegas crapshoot.

Rapid-Cycle Project Design

Choosing to pursue a rapid-cycle attack does not mean opting for the tactical instead of the strategic. When I am on a steep snowy slope, I want my ski instructor to provide some tips that I can translate into greater control right away. Also, I expect her to provide only as many instructions as I can absorb at once. Despite this focus on the immediate, however, neither of us, consultant or client, has lost the strategic view. We both know what an ideal skier looks like, and we both know that this is the goal that I, her client, am striving for. Why shouldn't an organization get from its consultants what I always get from my ski instructor—help that is not only immediately useful and achieves what must be accomplished at once but also moves the organization toward its more comprehensive goals.

On any consulting project there are almost always steps that can be taken to produce results and produce them quickly. Clients ought to insist that their consultants help them start this way. This chapter shows how large-scale projects can be carved into meaningful, productive, rapid-cycle subprojects. It also demonstrates that such subprojects, rather than obfuscating large-scale change strategies, actually provide fresh insight and momentum for them. For example, each of the initial rapid-cycle projects for the State of Connecticut, United Aluminum, and Motorola described in Chapters Three and Four contributed to the formulation of comprehensive change strategies for those clients.

Selecting rapid-cycle subprojects is not actually difficult to do; what is difficult is for clients and consultants used to the conventional mode to shift their thinking and embrace the idea. The selection of the first subproject or two is particularly important, because they will serve as momentum builders. Client and consultant first need to define the overall goals of the larger project; they can then carve out some shorter-term, stepping-stone goals. Sometimes a semiformal workshop can be organized to permit a larger number of key players to participate in considering and selecting the initial rapid-cycle projects.

Naturally, a rapid-cycle project must focus on the client's most urgent goals. There are four other criteria you might use in selecting the initial rapid-cycle projects:

1. *Short-term.* It should be possible to achieve measurable progress within ten or fifteen weeks.

2. *Focused on achieving measurable results.* As described in Chapter Four, the goal must be defined in bottom-line terms, and it must be something the client can measure.

3. *Matched to client readiness.* While the goal should be a real stretch for the people who have to achieve it, they should feel both able and willing to achieve it.

4. *Strategic.* The goal should clearly be a logical step toward achieving the client's overall goals. This makes certain that immediate progress will contribute to longer-term change and not simply win a momentary tactical advantage.

The Vitrine Products project described in Chapter Five illustrates a project that met the rapid-cycle criteria: the aim was to achieve a measurable step up in furnace efficiency of over 7 percent (a focus on achieving measurable results) within a few weeks (a short-term goal). Considerable effort was made to be certain that the goal would both represent a significant step beyond past performance and be achievable in the eyes of the furnace superintendent and his people (matched to client readiness). Finally, the project was a first step in implementing a major new strategic thrust, a multiyear performance improvement effort to be undertaken by the company that eventually returned many millions of dollars annually.

Laying a Foundation for Large-Scale Change

Here is how the Garrett Products Division of Group Dekko used rapid-cycle projects to launch a major turnaround.

Garrett was a profitable manufacturer of office lighting products. In 1995, however, the division began to experience difficulties. Its scrap rates rose and its on-time delivery declined. Profits suffered. Andy Barker, the division's general manager, launched several teams to study and correct the problems. They had some modest success, but not nearly as much as Barker wanted.

In thinking about what had happened, Barker realized that the difficulties resulted, in part, from Garrett's expansion into non-lighting products that introduced a number of new, and possibly distracting, challenges for his people. In addition, there was some ambiguity in Garrett's relationship with its largest customer, Custom Lights, which happens to be another division of Group Dekko. Barker is the general manager of Custom Lights as well as of Garrett. This dilemma was exacerbated by the fact that the newer non-lighting products were not nearly as profitable as the traditional lighting products.

If Barker had invited a conventional consultant to help resolve his problems and increase profitability, there is little doubt that the first step would be a number of studies. First, operational studies would be needed to determine the cause and cure of the quality and delivery problems. Next, strategic and market analyses would have to be conducted to determine the wisdom of continuing as two separate businesses and to see whether it made sense to continue manufacturing the new non-lighting line. Many months would elapse before management even had a chance to see the diagnoses and recommendations.

Instead of trying to understand and resolve all the issues at once, Barker, with the help of my associate Harlow Cohen, formed three teams, each with members from both companies and each charged with producing some measurable improvement within a few months. One team worked on resolving the problem of overlapping roles and responsibilities between the two companies with the aim of reducing indirect expense. The second team worked to simplify the ordering, production planning, and scheduling processes with the goal of reducing work-in-process inventory. The third team piloted ways to streamline selected steps within the overall order-to-shipment process to reduce the time required and to eliminate duplicate inventories. Within ninety days of launching the projects, the order cycle time shrank by more than 50 percent, from over six to under three days. Work-in-process inventory dropped by 25 percent. Overhead costs were decreased by about 15 percent. And quality defects declined by two-thirds.

Thus, the logic of conventional consulting was turned around. Instead of a long detailed study to decide on the "correct" strategies and actions, followed by an equally long process to try to implement and benefit from them, several rapid-cycle projects enabled Garrett to quickly return to its former level of profitability. Beyond these immediate results, the experience of working with the intercompany teams on these projects provided Barker with some fresh insights that enabled him to formulate a new strategic direction for the two companies, while continuing the rapid-cycle performance improvement process.

Changing organizational structure, modifying the measurement system, revising incentives or rewards, conducting training, or improving processes—these activities by themselves do not constitute rapid-cycle projects. They are only the support elements that are introduced to help achieve a result. Unless tied to tangible results, such support activities tend to dissipate energy and resources and achieve little or nothing. By contrast, shortening cycle time, reducing inventory, cutting costs, improving yields, and eliminating non-value-added work and the like are the primary focus of rapid-cycle projects.

Carving Off Rapid-Cycle Projects from Large-Scale Goals

The first challenge in designing for rapid-cycle success is to visualize how to divide large-scale diffuse goals and programs into incremental steps. Exhibit 6.1 lists a few ways to do it.

When I stress in my seminars the need for rapid-cycle breakthrough projects, the consultant participants often respond that that is exactly what they do. They break their large-scale projects into phases: the preliminary study, the detailed proposal, the first-step study, the creation of prototypes, and so on. But these are merely steps in a long process, not separate subprojects. The client is excluded and doesn't see a result until all the steps have been completed.

A rapid-cycle subproject moves quickly through all the phases from start to finish, at which point an actual, measurable client goal

EXHIBIT 6.1. Carving Off Rapid-Cycle Projects.

1. If there are many dimensions that must be changed, start with only one or a few of them.
2. If there are many units to improve, start with only one or a few of them.
3. If major reengineering is the aim, start with one or a few subprocesses.
4. Get the present system or technology to produce better results instead of waiting years to revolutionize or replace it.
5. If groups in the client organization are "not ready" to proceed because of some delaying issue, use your ingenuity to find a piece to get moving on.
6. When the clients are focused on large-scale, long-term goals, carve off an achievable step toward those goals.
7. Even if it seems impossible to carve off a first-step goal, design and conduct an initial rapid-cycle test project nevertheless.

has been accomplished. That is not the same as dividing a large project into phases. A number of illustrations of how the methods listed in Exhibit 6.1 can be employed are provided on the following pages.

1.   *If there are many dimensions that must be changed, start with only one or a few of them.*

The systems group in the Hartford Insurance Company's Commercial Lines Group was facing a twenty-six-person-year backlog. The group seemed to be trapped forever in maintenance catch-up and never had a chance to develop the new systems the division needed to automate its operations. They had carried out a great many activities-type improvement efforts with no impact on the backlog.

Consultant Robert Neiman helped them conduct the following project. The department's senior managers selected three of its work groups and charged each group with achieving a 25 percent increase in productivity within the next three months. Each team leader was free to choose the approach they would use in the experiment and to use consulting support as needed.

The narrow focus at last gave them something they could successfully attack; and their subsequent success shed light on how they could keep the effort moving.

2.   *If there are many units to improve, start with only one or a few of them.*

Dun & Bradstreet's Information Services Division needed to revitalize the entire business. Douglas Smith, who was a McKinsey & Company partner at the time, describes the situation in his book *Taking Charge of Change:*

Dun & Bradstreet's Information Services Division (DBIS) gives its customers a plethora of information and analysis about millions of businesses. The company's credit report is so well known that many people even refer to competitive products as "D&B's."

When Ron Glover became president of DBIS in 1990, the warning signs of trouble were flashing. Financial performance had dipped after decades of predictable growth. Internally, the heads of various functions were so powerful that they literally considered their individual parts of DBIS as separate companies and rarely communicated with one another. A culture of isolation and relentless profit pressure had taken its toll.

That spring, Ron asked Mike Berkin to introduce total quality management to DBIS. Mike began with steps common to most TQM programs.[1]

There were a number of months of research and training. More than two hundred managers participated in intensive training sessions. At that point, Berkin wanted to get moving toward achieving results. Berkin described it to me this way:

I wanted to produce some real results. Our people didn't have to be convinced that something needed to be done. And I established some design points for the effort. We wanted an approach that was easy to understand; that would not require more investment in training or anything else until we began to see some results; that would be fun, that people would enjoy doing; and that we could do quietly and have some success and let the word slip out gradually rather than make any big splashes. There were too many cynics ready to pounce.

This was a rare occurrence: the client was demanding high-leverage, rapid-cycle consulting. Douglas Smith invited Charles Baum to play an active role in helping Berkin get moving toward his goals. Berkin describes the experience this way:

Doug and Charlie said we should do four or five or six projects to try it out. They did not want to have us gamble on doing just a few. Since the projects were all achievable in a short time and the approach was focused and hard-hitting, we did not mind doing that number. We chose eight projects in different functions where the rest of the business would be impressed if there was some success and where there would be some specific business gains to be made—not like working out the color combination for the dining room, which some quality programs I know about have done. And we picked leaders for those projects with the help of Charlie and Doug to make sure these initial projects were loaded for success.

So Berkin began with eight projects that he was certain could be carried out successfully and quickly. That confidence is the key, not the exact number of projects to be launched.

3. *If major reengineering is the aim, start with one or a few subprocesses.*

Large-scale reengineering projects typically manifest all of consulting's five frequently fatal flaws. Here is how consultant Elaine Mandrish helped a major electric utility company carve off a rapid-cycle subproject from a large-scale reengineering project.

One of its generating plants had been having serious problems with its equipment maintenance. Besides having a huge backlog of work, when the maintenance staff finally got to the jobs, more than 25 percent of the time the repair plan was incorrect or the needed parts were not available.

For two years the plant had been trying to reengineer its maintenance process to correct the problems, but they had not been able to dedicate key resources for months on end to complete the reengineered design. Then the new plant manager decided to stop trying to reengineer the whole process at once. Instead he and his management team identified maintenance planning as the major bottleneck. They set an objective to redesign the planning process so that for 95 percent of all jobs the parts would be available and the job completed on time.

A group of ten people representing all the relevant functions was brought together in a two-day workshop. They first mapped the current process on a white board, using self-sticking note sheets to describe each main step and ink markers to show the flow of work.

When team members saw how the process really worked, they were appalled. It was obviously too complex, with too many hand-offs, too much paper, and too many checkpoints. Too many people were involved in approving the plans and no one was clearly accountable for the process.

With the benefit of these insights, the team turned to a new white board and created a template for how the process ought to work. They eliminated most of the hand-offs and approvals and made a small cross-functional team responsible for planning each major job.

In addition, the process mapping had shown that while more than 60 percent of the maintenance jobs were very simple, the same complex planning process was followed for these as for the more complex jobs. For these they recommended substitution of a simple three-page document to guide the maintenance staff.

At the end of the workshop the team presented their recommended redesign to the senior plant management team and obtained approval to proceed. Within a few months the team carried out the steps needed to implement their plan.

The new process not only reduced the backlog significantly, but also is saving the plant millions of dollars a year. In a subsequent external audit, the new process and the teamwork involved in it were cited as key strengths of the plant.[2]

Results-driven process redesign also differs from reengineering in its approach to infrastructure and organizational changes. With standard reengineering, such changes are done on a large scale. With results-driven process redesign, they are done only as needed.

4. *Get the present system or technology to produce better results instead of waiting years to revolutionize or replace it.*

The 74th Street Station of the Consolidated Edison Company in New York City is equipped with six "package boilers" which can produce steam within several hours of start-up. This permits flexibility in responding to changing customer demand. The station's large boilers have to run all the time, and they require at least twenty-four hours to be turned off or on.

The package boilers are all quite old, however, and to achieve their purpose they have to be able to run reliably and in conformance with stringent environmental regulations. If they violate any environmental regulation, they must be pulled off-line. In order to ensure reliability, the plant's managers decided that new electronic controls were needed on these boilers.

To design and install such controls was going to require at least a year, and the present mode was intolerable to management. Consultant Keith Michaelson suggested trying to reduce the environmental operating problems right away. Since the plant had previously had some success on similar projects, the managers agreed to try. They had been experiencing two or three costly and inconvenient shutdowns a week; they set a goal of less than one per week.

They identified the most vulnerable points in their operating procedures and then worked on how to minimize those risks. For example, they saw that the greatest danger of opacity (dark smoke) occurred when starting up a package boiler. So a team of operating and maintenance people would meet at dawn each day to make certain that the start-up was done properly. They did all this planning and modifying of their operating methods during their first month of work.

They had only two incidents during the entire second month, an improvement far beyond their goal. Now they had confidence that they would be able to operate reliably for the year or more it would take to install the new controls. They also discovered that some of their ideas about what the electronic controls would accomplish were illusions. A number of the potential pollution factors would have to be controlled through better operations. Instead of waiting a year to discover this, they were able to put the knowledge to work at once.

5. *If groups in the client organization are "not ready" to proceed because of some delaying issue, use your ingenuity to find a piece to get moving on.*

It is not uncommon for managers to be reluctant to venture into rapid-cycle breakthrough projects. One reason is that as soon as they select a specific goal and commit themselves to achieving it, they are exposed to the possibility of failing. It may be safer to study the situation and delay taking action. Of course, this pattern matches perfectly the conventional consultant's inclination to conduct all the preliminaries before getting on with the main event. So both parties conspire—unconsciously, of course—to extend the preliminaries so that the day of reckoning is delayed.

To shake that pattern requires considerable dedication and creativity:

Some years ago, when working with an acquired Northern Telecom subsidiary, my firm discovered that the unit's inventory levels were out of control. The unit's officers asserted that they knew the situation was bad, but they couldn't deal with it until they got their new inventory tracking and control system installed. Even though completion of the new system was still many months away, the managers insisted that there was no way to take any effective action. "We don't even know how much inventory we have, nor where it is," they said, "so how can we do anything to reduce it?"

Refusing to give up, a dauntless, results-focused consultant kept probing and eventually discovered that there were certain categories of inventory that management had more information about than others. In fact, there was one category for which management had a very good sense of both the amount and location. It was called SNA, that is, "shipped but not accepted." The company manufactured complex electronic products. When customers believed that a newly installed product's performance was inadequate, they didn't pay the invoice. This equipment remained on the company's books as part of its inventory. This was a serious customer relations as well as inventory control problem.

The consultant suggested a way to lower SNA inventory by solving the quality problems and getting the customers to pay. It had never occurred to management that they could deal with a single category of inventory, but they were more than willing to try it. As is usual in such projects, they were able to make some significant progress in a matter of weeks. Not only were they able to reduce SNA inventory (and the associated customer complaints), but the experience provided some fresh insights on how to strengthen the inventory control system then being constructed.

6. *When the clients are focused on large-scale, long-term goals, carve off an achievable step toward those goals.*

The General Reinsurance Corporation (General Re) provides a variety of risk-transfer mechanisms and other services to insurance companies. Traditionally, each General Re client company was contacted independently by a variety of General Re specialists, each responsible for one kind of reinsurance the client had purchased (or might purchase). In 1992, senior management decided that to provide the best possible service to their clients, teams representing all of General Re's specialties should be formed to provide integrated support for each client. It was planned that once the switch was thrown, hundreds of such teams would be formed—a monumental transition.

My firm was working with the company to support this process. We encouraged the company to select a few clients and test the idea before throwing the switch. Six clients and two potential clients were selected, and a team was assembled for each. Without too much concern for spelling out the ground rules in advance, team members were given some brief training and were asked to identify a few critical goals they could accomplish in ten or twelve weeks. We carefully documented each team's work. Instead of devoting three months to studying what such teams *might* produce, we simply had a number of teams get to work—and they accomplished some important gains, both with active clients and with prospects. They gained a wealth of practical experience, and the experiment provided senior management with sufficient confidence to move forward with the project.

General Reinsurance's experience demonstrates that no matter how complex or far-reaching a client's goal, it is always possible to carve off some rapid-cycle steps. For example, instead of undertaking a formal study of whether to design and market a new product, find a way to simulate the product, or buy it from another supplier, and try selling it (at what you think will be the appropriate market price) in one test market. Or carve off one element of a broad strategic plan and make it work over the short term in one place.

A number of years ago, a number of engineers in the division of Motorola that manufactures portable radios (such as those carried by security people) got the idea that fast-food restaurants would provide a large market if the division could develop the right kind of radio. Together with their results-focused consultant, the engineers decided that the company's formal new-product-proposal pathway would take too long. Instead, they took a few samples of a current product, made some quick fixes to it in their shop, and took these informal prototypes out to a local fast-food restaurant to test their idea. And, as is said, the rest is history. This project clearly demonstrated that zest can be injected even into strategic projects that are long-term and large-scale.

7. *Even if it seems impossible to carve off a first-step goal, design and conduct an initial rapid-cycle test project nevertheless.*

Sometimes both the client and the consultant are absolutely convinced that there is no way to divide a huge project into increments.

I believe that even in these cases, clients and consultants who have never produced significant results together should try to avoid the big gamble of a big project. Instead, the parties should invent a short-term project that is akin to, even if not exactly a part of, the proposed big project, to gain experience working together. In a few months, both parties will know how well they work together, and if they decide to move ahead to the large-scale job, they will be more clear about how to ensure success.

One example of such a project was suggested to me at a meeting of information-technology executives representing various units of a very large corporation. I was expounding the merits of rapid-cycle design to them when one of the participants interrupted me. "The concept is a good one, Robert, but you probably don't understand how systems projects work. There is no such thing as an incremental step. Projects require a minimum of six or nine months, or even much longer." Before I could say anything, another participant rose and responded as follows:

> Yes, that may be true. But let me tell you about a time when we were called into [a company's] plant to work on their inventory management system. The problem was in raw materials inventory. They had too much inventory overall but also suffered from frequent stock-outs. It seemed clear that we would have to revamp the entire system and that it would take many months. Before trying to lay out a design, we spent some time chatting with people in the plant, trying to get a sense of how the place worked. And we discovered one reason for their problems.
>
> Following these interviews, we drafted a letter for the plant manager to send to all of the plant's vendors, telling them that if they wanted to remain on the approved vendor list, they should sign and return a copy of the letter, indicating they would conform with its requirements. The letter specified six vital pieces of information that were to be (a) listed in any paperwork accompanying (or electronic communications about) any order and (b) plainly printed on the outside of anything shipped to the plant. That one step went a long way

toward solving their immediate raw materials inventory crisis, and it provided some important perspective on the system we were going to develop.

Someone asked how long it took to do that. The answer was three days. While this project did not result in much client learning, it does demonstrate that there is almost always a way to carve out a rapid-cycle project.

Even in cases where large studies with long cycle times seem to be necessary, it is often possible to carve off some preliminary projects and carry them forward while the big study is getting under way. And sometimes a series of action projects, each a mini experiment, testing some new approach or mode of operating, can actually substitute for a costly up-front study.

Using Quick Successes to Energize Strategic Change

In any rapid-cycle project, a key goal is to make some tangible progress rapidly, instead of requiring management to wait many months. The measurable results are only one dimension of the outcome. As in the case of the Consolidated Edison package boilers and Dun & Bradstreet's Information Services business, the lessons learned in the first rapid-cycle projects provide important experience for both client and consultant on how to shape more ambitious strategic steps. The rapid-cycle approach permits clients to adopt the consultant's contributions a step at a time, absorbing what they are capable of absorbing and all the while producing tangible bottom-line improvements.

Also, in order to make a consultant's contributions work well in an organization, many associated changes must take place in concert with the consultant's recommended steps. The initial rapid-cycle projects enable clients to learn how to manage these changes. A succession of rapid-cycle projects gives clients and consultants opportunities to move through the entire implementation cycle many times, with each implementation producing better results than the last. That is obviously much safer than the conventional game, where all your chips are on the table for a single roll of the dice.

7

Build a Partnership to Achieve and to Learn

Two days after attending a meeting on improving order processing at MVE, Inc., of Bloomington, Minnesota, Karen Prasch, a customer service specialist, sent a three-page letter to the person who had run the meeting: J. David O'Halloran, the company's president and, at that time, chief financial officer. Prasch was responsible for processing orders from all over the world for the company's cryogenic bulk tanks. Each order had many unique customer-dictated specifications, and this was further complicated by each country's special regulations for the importation of these vacuum tanks. The letter began by saying, "I left the meeting feeling angry and disappointed because the original goal of our group was not addressed." It continued by outlining many things that were going wrong with the handling of international orders. Prasch, who wanted so much to do a good job, was frustrated because she couldn't see what she could do to improve the situation beyond urging others to take action.

The list of problems outlined in her letter would have served as an open invitation to a lengthy, complex conventional consulting approach. The situation seemed to require a variety of studies to diagnose what was wrong with the order entry process. A set of recommendations would then have to be created. These would have to be reviewed with the client.

Finally, some months later, the consultants would have to send in a team to implement the recommendations, since no one in MVE had much experience with process redesign.

Instead, with the help of my associate Claude Guay, just a few weeks later Prasch was leading a work session with managers and employees from product management, engineering, finance, and traffic. After exploring the problems to be dealt with, they set an initial goal of correctly entering each order within twenty-four hours, instead of the several weeks it was then sometimes taking. They began creating a map of the process for international bulk tank orders. The process mapping revealed that there were certain items, such as documentation packages, that could be attacked at once, while more complex issues would have to be addressed later.

In their effort to reduce order entry time to one day, they also reduced the time required for customer service representatives to enter orders. They improved the accuracy of freight quotes, and they reduced the number of missed shipping dates. Step by step, they attacked the main goal and a number of related ones. Gradually the turnaround time was reduced to about a day, while many other improvements were also occurring. The customer service group gradually developed the ability to process twice as many orders with the same number of people while translating customer orders into manufacturing specs with greater accuracy.

This was the beginning of an effort that grew into a continuing program of improvement in the company's order entry and related processes for a variety of products. As the work advanced, Prasch enlisted employees and managers from every related function to participate in the work of her team. And she initiated several new teams led by her or other team members.

Guay helped her gradually develop skill in organizing work teams, leading process mapping and process redesign workshops, and project management. She became an effective facilitator and discovered that she could have an enormous impact on introducing change and affecting bottom-line results. She felt justifiably proud and enjoyed a succession of successes. Her confidence expanded along with her skills.

All of the work on this project was done within a partnership between a consultant with over twenty years of experience in performance improvement and a client who had extensive knowledge of the workings of the targeted system but virtually no team leadership or project experience. The process mapping was done in collaboration. The action steps were planned and executed in collaboration. Guay shared insights and skills with Prasch and her associates. Sometimes Guay functioned as a member of a working team. Sometimes he simply helped various team leaders plan their work sessions. Sometimes Guay did some of the work that had to be done. The main goal was to maximize learning by MVE people and have MVE people do as much of the work as possible. A parallel effort, headed by Lois Tuma, was carried out in another product area. As they developed new skills on both of the projects, various team members went off and initiated their own improvement team projects on their own. Meanwhile, Guay worked in the same flexible way with several of those teams.

On each of the projects there was a strong focus on results from the very beginning. The work began with several rapid-cycle projects matched to what the clients had said they were ready and able to carry out. The projects were successful. Beyond these tangible gains, the twenty or thirty people who participated in these projects learned more from their successful experiences in producing results than they might have learned in a dozen training courses. As a consequence, the company now possesses staff who have abilities in process mapping and redesign, team leadership, goal setting, and project planning that can be exploited in the years ahead.

Learning Through Collaboration

The MVE case illustrates how a consulting project can serve as a rich opportunity for developing clients' capabilities. The most effective way to exploit this learning opportunity is for the client and consultant to work closely together in a partnership mode. Both should share in performing any research that is needed as well as in analyzing the findings, deciding on the appropriate course of action, and implementing it to produce results. This is what Claude Guay did in working with MVE. The approach must be expanded on larger-scale projects, but the basic concept is the same.

One reason for the rapid-cycle design, in fact, is to provide repeated opportunities for the client-consultant partnership to move through the entire project cycle. That means beginning a project, carrying it through to success, and learning from it.

This partnership approach overcomes a major deficiency of conventional consulting, that the consultant does the work and presents a finished product to the client. As described earlier in this book, that mode limits clients' ability to develop their capabilities in the course of a project. The consultants debate the issues and work out their doubts and confusions before presenting their conclusions to the client. Since much learning comes from the process of speculation and discovery, the hand-off mode guarantees that the consulting team will learn much and the client staff little.

High-impact consulting is predicated on the belief that a change project offers a rich range of potential learning experiences for both the client and the consultant, and projects need to be designed to exploit those opportunities.

Managing Projects in the Partnership Mode

To get into a partnership frame of mind, clients and consultants have to abandon the traditional view that a consulting project is essentially a task carried out by a consultant on behalf of a client. Instead, the project has to be seen as a joint undertaking to produce a joint product. Moreover, both players have to accept the fact that much of the work that large consulting teams carry out can and should be done by client personnel. If they do it, they will not only produce greater results for less expense, they will also benefit from the learning that results from the experience.

The project described below, for Morgan Bank's Administrative Services Department, illustrates well how the partnership mode works and how projects can be designed to serve as development vehicles for client staff.

When Bill Hayes assumed responsibility for the Administrative Services Department at Morgan Bank in the mid 1980s, he decided that there was no justification for the other bank departments to continue spending $90 million a year for administrative services they might not want or could obtain in a less costly manner elsewhere. Therefore, he made the department's forty-plus unit managers responsible for "selling" their services to the other bank departments and negotiating fees for them. Hayes told his people that their units' survival required major improvements in performance and customer responsiveness.

To communicate his view of the importance of producing measurable results for their customers, Hayes convened his managers in a workshop and asked each of them to identify one important, measurable, short-term service improvement they could accomplish in the next few months with some consulting assistance. How these goals were translated into results is illustrated by the experience of Dorothy Jacobson, head of the Micrographics Department.

Jacobson's unit was responsible for transferring to microfilm from computer tapes the daily operating data of every department in the bank. Her unit promised twenty-four-hour turnaround service but rarely met that goal. Jacobson was told she had to start meeting the target. With the consultant's help, Jacobson carved off a first-step, rapid-cycle goal: within five weeks, her unit would regularly meet the twenty-four-hour deadline for a single bank department, known as 30 West Broadway.

Jacobson started by drafting an assignment memo to her key assistant, John Palladino, outlining the 30 West Broadway goal and asking him to give her a draft action plan in writing outlining the specific steps that he and his people would carry out to achieve the goal. When Palladino voiced his skepticism that the goal could be reached without additional people and resources, Jacobson restated her resolve. "I understand that this appears to be difficult," she said, "but we're going to take this one step at a time. Expectations have been raised. We're not working at the same level anymore."

Palladino's action plan was put in place and key personnel were prepped on their new responsibilities. During the very first week of the project, the computer tapes from 30 West Broadway were misplaced for a day. Jacobson used this mishap to fashion some new procedures for the unit. First, she named one supervisor on each shift to take on a new role, "work flow coordinator." Every job was tracked throughout the three operating shifts. In addition, she created a temporary structure, called the supervisor action committee, to resolve conflicts between the shifts. Finally, she created a wall chart to track the results of all work coming from 30 West Broadway. This allowed everyone in the unit to know on a daily basis how quickly work was getting completed and what progress was being made toward accomplishing the turnaround goal.

The consultants spent some time each week with Jacobson, Palladino, and the other active participants. As with the MVE case, they provided some expert inputs, but more importantly, they helped the client managers think through for themselves what they had to do to achieve their goal. The consultants provided ideas about tools and procedures the client might want to try. As the weeks passed, the number of days for which the twenty-four-hour goal was met increased, and people's confidence in working together to meet deadlines grew. At the end of the five weeks, the challenge had been met: 30 West Broadway was being turned around on a twenty-four-hour basis every day.

The effort left an indelible mark on the unit and its people. They had responded to a demand that they once considered impossible. In doing so, they had set and met goals, redesigned the flow of work in their department, refined the way people worked together, modified the organizational structure, and increased the amount of responsibility the department's people carried. Most important, they now believed in their own ability to tackle a difficult assignment and produce results. And they were prepared to move to the next goal: satisfying their other customers.

The consultant had not only helped Jacobson and her people accomplish a specific, measurable performance improvement but had helped them develop the capacity to sustain the improvement process and implement other improvements in the future. This kind of learning and development, irrelevant to so much management consulting, is not merely an incidental benefit of high-impact consulting; it is a central ingredient. Every consulting project offers a rich array of such opportunity for helping clients to expand their skills and insights. Although the twenty-four-hour project was focused on a very specific goal, many opportunities for development were exploited. Here are the most important ones:

1. *Diagnosing readiness*. During the kickoff workshop, Jacobson was introduced to the concept of selecting a goal that she could be pretty certain her people would accomplish. After some thought about what might actually be achieved in a rapid-cycle mode, she decided to limit her first goal to just 30 West Broadway.

When she left the workshop, she and the consultant had several conversations about how she could push for a goal that seemed impossible but that she gradually discovered could be achieved.

2. *Carving off achievable goals within a larger strategic framework*. For Dorothy Jacobson and her people, the overall goal of meeting the twenty-four-hour turnaround time on microfilm delivery was not something they could "get their arms around." It was just an

unfathomable burden. With what she learned from the workshop and from follow-up help from the consultant, however, she and her colleagues in the department translated the turnaround-time goal into a series of subgoals, each with a start date, an end date, and a measurable outcome.

Many management groups faced with large-scale challenges don't have experience in carving off a series of achievable subgoals. Learning this skill is important, because when management groups survey the totality of a large-scale challenge, it can seem overwhelming. The consultant spent time with Jacobson and her people thinking through appropriate ways to carve the overall project into achievable steps.

3.   *Framing demands for goal accomplishment.* Managers may be hampered in achieving their goals because they are not experienced or confident in communicating with their people about major improvements that must be achieved.

To make her project succeed, Dorothy Jacobson had to convey to her associates not that it would be *nice* to achieve their goal but that they *must* achieve it. She had a number of conversations with the consultant about making this shift. It was necessary for her to recognize that she had a number of anxieties about making demands and that she had to learn how to overcome them in working with her people on performance improvement.

4.   *Improving performance through an action-oriented, experimental approach.* Like the forty or so other managers in the bank's administrative services department, Jacobson was overwhelmed at first by the department head's demand for major performance improvement. In that she was no different from most mangers, who are sincerely doing the best they know how to do. Thus, when confronted by a demand for major improvements, they naturally feel that the goals are impossible.

The consultants introduced Jacobson and her fellow managers to the concept of focusing on short-term, manageable steps that begin to move a unit toward its broader goals and also permit the managers to learn as they go. The consultants worked along with the managers, intermittently, to help them design and carry out their projects. This required a few hours a week of consulting for several months. The aim was clearly for the unit managers to carry out the work on their own as they felt able to do so.

5.   *Involving people in performance improvement.* No matter how good a change idea or improvement recommendation may be, managers need to learn how to engage their people in planning the changes and carrying them out. The consultants helped Jacobson and Palladino experiment with some innovative ways to communicate with their people and bring them into active participation on the project. Here the consultants could provide a "menu" of ways this could be done, suggesting different ways meetings could be held and different ways people could play a role in the project.

The consultant also helped Jacobson and Palladino take the initiative in scheduling meetings with and reporting to some of the senior officers who were managing the improvement effort. Previously they had shared the view common to most middle managers: "when the boss wants to talk with me, he or she will call me." They developed the confidence to take the initiative when that seemed to make sense.

6.   *Developing work planning and project management skills.* Many managers lack well-developed skills in managing change. Such skills are essential to implementing the work of a consulting project. Therefore, consultants who want their clients to succeed must help them develop skills in project planning and management. These include determining how a project will be organized, how it will be managed, and how it will be carried out. It means learning how to work with groups of peers, subordinates, and consultants to create disciplined work plans that show in detail what is to be done, with timetables listing milestones to be reached along the way.

Is there a need for a steering group or groups? Are the tasks to be carried out by individuals? by small task groups? What is to be the pattern for project progress reviews? Who should participate in the reviews? How often should they be held? Who should be there? What should the format be? Who should be informed about project progress along the way? What should be done if the project does not stay on course? These were the critical questions the Micrographics people had to answer.

The consultants helped Jacobson and each of her key associates master the skills of breaking a task apart into steps and then assigning responsibility and accountability for each step. John Palladino and the various supervisors developed individual work plans. By using a wall chart to track the daily progress of jobs through the unit, Jacobson learned how powerful such tools can be in organizing and coordinating the work of a large group of people. Finally, Jacobson and Palladino both learned how to become the masters of their time rather the victims of random pressures. By creating and sticking with their project work plan, they avoided the distractions that sidetrack most managers.

7. *Dealing with conflicts, frustrations, and disappointments*. No manager who attempts to improve performance and accelerate the pace of progress can entirely avoid obstacles along the way. When they meet an obstacle, should they tough it out and push forward? When does it make more sense to pause, regroup, and possibly change the direction or design of the project? How can a manager deal with resistant associates in a way that is supportive but also maintains the integrity of the project?

Jacobson and Palladino faced considerable resistance. The people in the department felt they were already doing the best they could with the equipment and staff available to them. The twenty-four-hour goal seemed impossible to them. The opportunity to talk about her reaction to this kind of resistance with the consultant and overcome her unease about confronting it was one of the most important experiences for Jacobson.

8. *Working with a consulting resource*. Management consultants spend their entire professional lives working with client managers, but many managers only rarely or never work with consultants. It shouldn't be surprising, then, that most managers are uncertain about how to properly manage a consulting relationship. Yet having the client playing a strong contributing role is critical to designing and carrying out a successful project.

At the beginning of the microfilm project, Jacobson, Palladino, and their associates seemed to be waiting for instructions from the consultants. The consultants were explicit about the partnership mode and, by word and deed, showed what that meant. The managers became increasingly comfortable about asserting their views, declaring what kind of help they wanted from the consultants, and playing an increasingly active, leading role on the project.

9.   *Modifying organizational structures*. Managers often fantasize that having a better organizational structure or a better person on the job will solve their problems. Some managers make organizational changes frequently, always hoping that such changes will magically provide the rewards they hope for. In a results-driven improvement process, however, managers are encouraged not to view structural changes or shifting assignments as the answer to making change occur. Those interventions should instead be viewed as two possible actions to support all the other steps being taken.

In the Morgan Bank case, for example, after they had achieved tangible progress on a variety of innovations, Jacobson and her people decided that several organizational shifts would help speed progress. Thus they created the work flow coordinator position and supervisor action committee, described above. The consultant spent some time discussing the pros and cons of various moves and sharing parallel experiences in other organizations so that Jacobson and Palladino could sharpen their judgments about the sequencing of various change efforts.

10.   *Teaching the consultant's expertise*. A fundamental obligation of the consultant is to teach members of the client organization as much as possible about the subject matter the consultant has been engaged to address. This requires different levels of effort for different people: major effort with the specialists who will be responsible for maintaining the techniques or technologies within the organization, and lesser effort with the managers who will have to use the techniques or technologies or implement the consultants' recommendations.

One of the specific skills Jacobson and her key managers learned from the consultants in pursuing the twenty-four-hour turnaround goal was process redesign. They used these skills to differentiate between steps that were essential for getting the work accomplished and steps that could be eliminated. Process mapping was another specific skill Claude Guay brought to the MVE project. By collaborating with participants, he helped them learn to do it themselves.

Gunn Partners, a consulting firm that specializes in working with corporate staff functions, makes it a top priority to train client staff to play a major role in any project. Bob Moore, vice president and comptroller of the Union Camp Corporation, had this to say about the firm: "Conventional consultants want to be treated as the experts coming in to straighten us out. With them it is basically an adult-child relationship. With Gunn it was adult to adult partnership." Frank Rabil, manager of business processes for the company, commented, "So far we've saved about $5 million a year, with another $20 million identified. The consulting fees were only a small fraction of that. In addition, the consultants helped me to learn how to do business process redesign, and I will be working with the other divisions around the corporation to implement redesign. So we have developed internal capability as a result of the collaboration." And Jack Harrin, assistant comptroller, said, "The twelve people on the original pilot team all grew so much in stature and confidence. They have new perspectives on how work can get done."

One thing is for sure: if client learning is a key goal of the project, then the techniques and approaches the client is to learn need to be introduced at an appropriate pace. In Morgan Bank's microfilm department, people were trained in a "just-in-time" mode. Rather than dumping a huge load of new concepts on them in a training course, the consultants helped them learn new processes and procedures when that knowledge was needed to meet the challenge at hand. This strategy presents a dilemma for the large consulting organization that wants to shift to high-impact consulting. Large consulting teams, by their very nature, generate tons of material, often indigestible, that in the conventional consulting mode are delivered all at once at the conclusion of a project.

High-impact consulting is all about achieving results quickly while also learning how to achieve even more results, through a partnership relationship. The Morgan Bank and MVE examples show how a partnership approach can extend through every phase of a consulting project and focus on many learning dimensions.

While the microfilm project moved forward, over one hundred other Morgan Bank administrative services managers were carrying out parallel results-driven improvement efforts similar to Dorothy Jacobson's. Not only were most of their goals realized, saving many millions of dollars a year for the bank, but hundreds of people learned a whole array of new skills and techniques that equipped them to carry on.

Any client who fails to receive these benefits in the course of a consulting project is being cheated by the consulting process. Any consultants who fail to make this kind of learning integral to their work confine themselves to a sterile practice, barren of the joyful experiences that come from seeing one's clients learning and growing as well as achieving results.

Developing Learning Organizations

This results-based approach to managerial and organizational development is quite different from that advocated in a spate of recent writings on the subject of "the learning organization." A number of authors have usefully called attention to the fact that, in this time of ever-accelerating change, the only way organizations will keep pace is by providing opportunity for constant learning by their members. It is not enough for organizations to perform well. Since tomorrow's requirements are certain to be very different from today's, the leadership of organizations must devote major attention to making certain that their people learn what they will need to know in order to succeed in the future.[1]

These authors are making an important argument—that constant learning by its people must be a critical goal of every organization.

These writings on the learning organization, however, slight the importance of results-focused experiential learning. The authors tend to succumb to the same belief about change as conventional consultants—the idea that the right concepts, if properly communicated, will somehow exert so much power that organizations will find them inexorable. This view is illustrated in the following quotation by David Garvin: "Organizational learning can usually be traced through three overlapping stages. The first step is cognitive. Members of the organization are exposed to new ideas, expand their knowledge, and begin to think differently. The second step is behavioral. Employees begin to internalize new insights and alter their behavior. And the third step is performance improvement, with changes in behavior leading to measurable improvements in results: superior quality, better delivery, increased market share, or other tangible gains."[2]

This thinking is based on the belief that cognitive change (insight and knowledge) leads to behavioral change, which in turn leads to results. There is an apparent lack of appreciation of the fact that setting and achieving sharply defined, challenging goals—and learning from the experience, as Dorothy Jacobson did—and then doing it again, can be the most powerful vehicle for expanding an organization's capacity to set and achieve even more challenging goals. Peter Senge comes closest to an appreciation of experiential learning in his advocacy of "learning laboratories" and other simulations. He says that the effects of the learning laboratory can be seen most clearly when the managers implementing their learnings "focus first and foremost on business results." And he adds, "If they can find new approaches to enhance results, they will commit time and energy to them" and have more staying power than those turned on merely by the learning process.[3] My colleagues and I have found that life is the most exciting learning laboratory, and on-the-job experience is the most powerful.

To the extent that most of these writings on the learning organization refer to goals at all, they are mainly activity-based goals, such as, "improving actions," "correcting errors," "changing actions to reflect new insights," and so forth. The definitions do not reflect appreciation of the power of a challenging goal to trigger and energize the learning process. Garvin, in fact, seems to view interest in measurable results as possible evidence of short-sighted management: "Even half-life curves have an important weakness. They focus solely on results. Some types of knowledge take years to digest, with few visible changes in performance for long periods."[4] I don't deny that organizations must invest in critical long-term pursuits. Little learning occurs, however, in organizations that do not have frequent experiences setting goals and then mobilizing their wits and energies to achieve them.

Consultants Can Also Learn on the Job

While most managers and consultants would probably agree that consulting projects offer important opportunities for client learning, few appreciate the fact that there is much that consultants can learn on the job as well.

Consultants entering a new client situation (including internal consultants entering a new plant or department) are much like anthropologists exploring a culture that is new to them. Even though some of the artifacts, customs, and costumes may appear familiar, no anthropologist would assume that he or she understands a new culture on the basis of such evidence without careful study. And thus it should be with consultants. Oh yes, you have been in other large commercial banks. You may know that in a paper mill a blanket is not used for sleeping. You understand the odd patterns on your client's balance sheet. You grasp the exquisite delicacy of semiconductor manufacturing. You may have extensive expertise of all sorts, but in a new client relationship, you know very little about the unique and idiosyncratic dynamics of the client organization. And unless you put your assumptions on hold, you may fail to learn what you need to learn about how the organization actually works and what it will take to improve its performance.

Consultants need to ask questions about the workings of the client organization as well as about the technical issues the assignment raises. Here are some of the factors a consultant should investigate at the earliest possible moment:

1. How do things really work in this company? What has enabled them to get as far as they've gotten? What are the unique strengths and capabilities that current problems and difficulties might be obscuring?

2. Who are the people most open to new ideas and experimentation? Where can the most progress be achieved most quickly?

3. What are the relationships among key individuals and groups? What are the unique ways they have of working and interacting?

4. What might work here? What would be unlikely to work? Have I been in organizations like this before? What did I learn about the forces for and against change in those organizations?

These are the kinds of issues consultants need to understand in order to decide how to work with a client and in order to make certain their technical expertise is used most effectively. Developing insight into these issues should be one of the objectives of the readiness assessment.

There is also much to be learned by the consultant once the project begins to move forward:

1. When a commitment is made, is it honored by everyone in the organization?

2. How open to experimentation is the organization? Are there any taboo areas where they won't tread?

3. How do the people in the organization respond to consulting help? Do they see consultants as intruders or as helpers? What kinds of behavior by the consulting team elicits the best reactions from the client's people? Are we doing anything that turns them off or makes them resentful?

4. With respect to the specialized knowledge we have been asked to contribute, where does the client stand now? How well are

they using what they have? How much more do they really need? How much can they absorb at once?

5. Have we learned anything about the organization that suggests that we should review our original project design with the client and possibly modify it?

6. Are we identifying the organization's "tender spots," the issues certain key players are sensitive or defensive about? Are they experimenting with different ways of handling these delicate issues?

The more consultants learn about these matters, the more powerful their contributions will be. To develop these insights requires working with an organization for a while, attempting to make progress together, encountering and overcoming barriers, and learning from the experience.

If consultants work hard to learn about these issues during each individual project, they will also develop their overall grasp of how to facilitate change in organizations. The rapid-cycle approach, with repeated start-to-finish advances in a partnership mode, offers consultants numerous opportunities to develop insights into these vital issues. And with added insight comes greater ability to plan additional steps with more certainty.

Another dimension of this consultant learning is the development of effective working relationships with key client personnel. Over time a consultant can develop relationships that facilitate goal setting and action planning. Unfortunately for many clients, on-the-job learning and relationship building are irrelevant to those consultants who believe that their job is to deliver so many pounds of high-quality know-how. The following experience is not unique:

A very large, very well known consulting firm had a contingent of consultants working in a financial services company that was carrying out a major transformation affecting nearly every aspect of its operations. My firm was also working with the company, and I became aware that every once in a while, one of the other firm's consultants disappeared, never to be seen again. When I inquired, I was informed that they had been reassigned or rotated onto other accounts. After a few months on the job, each consultant would simply disappear, to be replaced by another equally bright, equally well dressed and well coiffured consultant. It was clear that their firm regarded them as interchangeable parts, valued for their knowledge and skills but not for anything they might learn about the client organization or any relationships they might develop with the client's people.

The concept of a client-consultant partnership was obviously meaningless to this firm. One of the easiest shifts a conventional consulting firm can make toward high-impact consulting is to accept the need to learn about each client organization and from each group of clients and to value relationships with the clients' people.

Project Assessment: Mutual Learning

Project progress review and assessment sessions are formal mechanisms for making certain that the client and consultant come together to assess what they are learning and decide how to benefit from that assessment. Here are the kinds of questions that should be on the review meeting agenda:

- Is the project proceeding according to plan?
- Is anything turning up that should cause us to consider changing the assumptions around which the project was designed?
- How do we feel about how we are working together? What is working best? What is working less well? Should we test some different ways of working together?
- Looking forward, do we still hold to the timetable and goals we set at the beginning of the project? Are we still as confident of achieving the results we said we would achieve?

- Are there people who are not in this meeting who need to be brought up-to-date on the project? Are there any who need to be consulted on how to proceed? Any whose help we may need but are not sure we can obtain?

To make these reviews most useful, people need to be encouraged to believe that no aspect of the project is immune from examination and modification. The leaders of these sessions should endeavor to make them as frank and open as possible. Clients should not have to strive to be polite in such sessions; their honest reactions to the project are valuable data. Consultants need to try to understand and deal with client doubts and concerns rather than try to answer them or explain them away.

Then, at the end of each project, a more extensive session should be held for the client and consultant to assess how well they accomplished what they intended to accomplish, both on the immediate project and in terms of making progress toward larger-scale, longer-term goals.

A few of the participants could be asked to prepare papers and presentations. In the partnership mode, it is often client people who make such presentations. Karen Prasch, for example, MVE's customer service specialist, made a number of presentations to senior management on the order processing project she was managing with the help of a consultant. Here are some of the questions that might be addressed in such a session:

- How much of what was intended did the project accomplish?
- What were some of the main lessons for the client about what it will take to continue to improve results and accelerate progress?
- How well did the client and consultant collaborate? Were their roles well spelled out, and did people carry out their roles as expected?
- If this project were to be carried out over again, how would we do it differently?

- What light was shed on the client's strategic goals and directions?
- What are the most potentially useful projects for the next step? Can strategic as well as operational advances be achieved in subsequent projects?

At the end of a project, clients are much more sophisticated about the specialized information and technology their consultants have introduced. They are more sophisticated about how to work with the consultant to manage change and improvements. The consultants have also learned much about how to contribute most effectively. All of this capability has more opportunity to develop in a series of rapid-cycle projects than with a single large-scale, once-around-the-track project.

Barriers to the Partnership Mode

The fact that client-consultant collaboration adds great value to a consulting project does not mean clients will automatically be eager to embrace the approach. They might insist that although they would love to do so, "My people just don't have the time." Or, "My people are all tied up with the new acquisition." Or, "We're right in the middle of year-end budgeting." Or, "Why do we need to pay a consultant if we have to do all the work?"

Actually, the time required for a client to participate responsibly can always be kept to a reasonable level. The client's participation is so valuable that consultants who pander to their clients' desire to dump the problem in the consultant's lap and quickly turn to other tasks are doing their clients a disservice.

In Chapter Four I described why both clients and consultants may feel more comfortable in the conventional mode, even if it produces fewer results. But managers will always pay a big price for hiding in the safety of the conventional consulting mode, with its formal presentations and meetings and back and forth hand-offs. Managers should freely reveal to the consultants they hire what they and their people know and don't know, and their consultants should help them identify what they need to learn. If they are the right consultants, they will do this in a fashion that does not threaten the managers (too much) or make them feel exposed.

And, of course, consultants feel most comfortable going off to "do their thing" on projects. To be more effective, however, they must work more closely with their clients. That is not easy. Consultants have to come to grips with their reluctance to adopt the role of change agent, collaborator, and coach. While there are conventional consultants who do some client coaching, too many are still uncomfortable in the role of change facilitator and are not strongly motivated to overcome that discomfort.

This was graphically illustrated to me in a visit to the Harvard Business School some years ago. I learned that about 800 of the 1,600 graduate students in residence belonged to the school's management consulting club. At that time, Professor Arthur Turner was offering a course on how to facilitate change in organizations. Only about ten of the 800 consulting-club members felt interested enough to sign up for the course. I dare say the same pattern would be repeated in most graduate business schools. These graduate students understand that they will be welcomed into a consulting firm if they learn as much as they can about every management subject other than change management.

High-leverage strategy, however, requires that the consultant help clients learn to carry out change. Thomas Kivlehan, vice president of reengineering at Simon & Schuster, captured the value of this kind of client-consultant partnership in describing his work with a firm that practices high-leverage consulting and places a very high value on developing a partnership with clients: "The capacity to manage change is one of the most valuable resources in any company today. When you work with a Gunn Partners type of consultant, you will be getting experience in how to make change happen, and you will become more skilled and feel more empowered to do so. It is an investment in your people. There is no training in the world that can substitute for that." This is quite different from serving up consultant wisdom or consulting products. It means providing continuous support as the client experiments with new modes. Since this is an unfamiliar role for most consultants, a good start for consulting firms would be to provide some training for their consultants who want to play such a role.

Only consultants who share a strong sense of responsibility for client successes or failures and who treat each consulting project as a valuable personal learning experience for themselves and their clients can hope to become effective partners with those clients.

8

Leverage Resources: More Results, Not More Consultants

As one facet of the broad effort to "reinvent the government" headed by Vice President Gore, the Occupational Safety and Health Administration in the Department of Labor engaged a consulting firm in 1994. Its mission: help identify core management processes and launch teams empowered to improve them.

> With OSHA staff assistance, the consulting firm identified five "core processes" and formed teams to improve each of them. The teams were given free rein to reinvent the way OSHA did things. The consulting firm provided training in quality improvement methods, problem solving, and group dynamics to representative groups from around the country. Early meetings focused on building teams, defining problems, collecting baseline data, creating a "quality story," and other typical activities-driven preparatory steps.
>
> Six months later, Assistant Secretary Joe Dear, the head of OSHA, convened the teams to review the ideas and recommendations they had developed. The groups had few results to report, however, and they were discouraged about their progress. As Rob Medlock, area director of the Cleveland office and a team leader, recalled,
>
> We were feeling pretty bad as a team because we had no tangible successes. The training we had gone through had laid down a very spe-

cific process. First you go through each of these steps, and at the end you reach a result. Then you evaluate the result. Then you start again. We were not allowed to circumvent the process, because each step led to the next. In theory, it was great. In practice, it was demotivating, because we had to spend so much time going through the steps before we could actually *do* anything. Remember, we continued working the whole time. The phones didn't stop ringing. We only had limited time, and most of it was spent on process, not making changes.

Coincidentally, as part of a broader redesign effort under way in the Department of Labor, consultant Charlie Baum was assigned to work with OSHA at just about that time. Baum was experienced with high-impact change techniques, and he and Joe Dear agreed to try a new tack. They decided to aim at a tangible success on one critical core process: reducing the time required for workers to eliminate workplace hazards called in to OSHA by workers. Instead of trying to reduce response time in all seventy area offices at once, one regional administrator, Mike Connors, volunteered to take the lead in two of his offices, Cleveland and Peoria. It was also agreed, despite some skepticism, to concentrate on only one of the two types of complaint processes. As Medlock recounted, "Charlie wanted to focus just on the nonformal complaint process. I was doubtful that would be useful. Our office already received more than one thousand such complaints each year, and we believed we were already experts in handling them."

Nevertheless, the team leaders agreed to test the nonformal complaint process first. Baum spent a day in each office, with teams led by the office director. Within an hour or so, the teams and Baum were able to map the workplace complaint process flow and use a fishbone exercise to identify several problems interfering with progress. Then, asked by Baum to define a goal in terms of results (instead of naming processes to improve), the two teams decided to try to reduce the average time it took an office to process a complaint by 25 percent within eight weeks. The teams then created action plans for achieving that goal.

With only telephone conferences with the consultant after the first day's workshop, the two offices began to experiment with alternative ways to process worker complaints. For example, instead of sending a formal letter filled with legalese to employers, they asked each complainant to provide a contact person and phone number at his or her company. Through same-day phone calls, OSHA staffers quickly notified employers of alleged problems. They then entered into open, relatively friendly discussions with employers about how the problems could be abated. Faxes were used to allow quicker back-and-forth communication with employers. Complainants retained all of their rights by being given the opportunity to verify abatement and to dispute the employer's response if they wished to do so.

By the end of the eight weeks, the Cleveland office had reduced the average time from receipt of an employee complaint to abatement of the condition from thirty-nine to nine working days. In Peoria the reduction was from twenty-three to five work days. Instead of the targeted 25 percent reduction, both offices achieved better than a 75 percent reduction. What is more, the OSHA employees who participated in the breakthrough process remember it as a time of learning, excitement, and growth. As Peggy Zweber, the Peoria office director and team leader, recalled, "It was the best thing that ever happened to this office! We worked as a team and accomplished so much. The most important thing was that each person's contribution was valued and treated with equal attention. There were six of us in the group, but I wish that everyone had been able to participate."

The project not only produced dramatic results but also laid the groundwork for rapid expansion of the improvement effort. After the first two successes, the process was rolled out across the country. Each regional office identified a senior "reinvention sponsor" who came to Washington for two days of training by Baum and key members of the Cleveland and Peoria teams. Nelson Reyneri, who headed up the reinvention effort, described the rollout: "Historically, we would have just sent out a memo, a compliance directive. We communicated just about everything that way. But we wanted the changes to be successful and to be lasting so we had the 'reinvention sponsors' come together personally. The great results in Cleveland and Peoria opened people's eyes to the possibility that they, too, could improve. The results have been excellent. The time to resolve nonformal complaints has been reduced by 70 percent across the country in the past year."

The amount of consulting support required to achieve the results in the Cleveland and Peoria offices was about three or four days of consulting per office. The amount required to support the national rollout was only an additional three to five days.

This project focused on measurable client results. It began with a rapid-cycle success. The pace and scope, although a significant stretch for the participants, was designed to match what they felt they could accomplish. It was carried out as a learning partnership between client and consultant. When all those factors are fully in play, a relatively small amount of consulting effort can produce tremendous results. The performance of seventy offices nationwide was affected by less than a month's work by a single consultant. That's why high-impact consulting is also highly leveraged consulting.

In the OSHA case as well as the cases described in earlier chapters, the more the clients "made it happen," the more they learned the techniques the consultants were trying to introduce. They learned about project management. They gathered data themselves, instead of having to trust the consultant's findings and reports. They leavened the project with insights about their organization's operations that the consultants could not possibly have possessed. And they developed the ability to sustain progress on ongoing projects and also to conduct new projects.

For all these reasons, even if high-impact consulting cost 50 or 100 percent more than conventional consulting, it would nevertheless be worth choosing it. But the wonderful thing is that high-impact consulting produces its results for only a fraction of the costs of labor-intensive conventional consulting.

Contrast the Department of Labor case with this one:

A successful financial services company that marketed to corporate rather than individual customers decided that its future success would require it to work more closely with its customers' managers. In order to define more accurately what their customers' requirements might be, the managers in charge of the transformation decided that in-depth interviews should be conducted with senior people in a number of customer companies. The consulting team helping to plan the new approach to customers supported this decision and devised an interview protocol.

When the question of who should do the interviews was raised, the consultants quickly suggested that customers might not speak freely to the company's own people. Moreover, the company's people, though skilled as salespeople, might not be sufficiently skilled to follow the interview protocol. They suggested that consultants should do the interviews, at least until they were certain of obtaining valid results. At a later time, they said, it might be useful to have some of the client company's own people do some interviews. It sounded so logical that the client's senior people agreed at once with the suggestion.

This incident exemplifies the way conventional, labor-intensive consultants view their roles. The consultants believed, correctly, that if they did the interviews they would be done well. They did not, however, consider the fact that their doing the interviews would rob the company's own people of the opportunity to develop new skills while also hearing firsthand what their customers were thinking. Moreover, the project cost the client much more than it needed to, since the consultants were used in the most labor-intensive fashion.

The work in a number of departments of the State of Connecticut described in Chapter Four illustrates the difference between labor-intensive conventional consulting and highly leveraged consulting. The project was a seven-year collaboration between external consultants and various facility managers and internal consultants. The project began yielding results almost at once, bucking the nearly universal trend of rising workers' compensation costs. Eventually the continuing savings grew to well over $10 million a year. Beyond those tangible results, there is now throughout the state a well-trained, experienced cadre of leaders and facilitators in place who are carrying the work forward.

At no time were more than three outside consultants engaged on the project, and they each worked half-time or less on it. The overall consulting fees for the entire seven years were less than $400,000. The project has yielded a continuing annual cash dividend amounting to twenty or thirty times the state's investment in consulting and a group of knowledgeable leaders and facilitators to sustain the process. That is highly leveraged consulting.

Moving Toward Highly Leveraged Consulting

If you want to see what the highly leveraged approach might contribute to your situation, whether you are a client or a consultant, here is some "how-to" advice to consider:

1. *Help clients see the value of leveraged consulting compared to labor-intensive consulting.* For clients, the first step is to understand the benefits and challenges of highly leveraged consulting and then insist that your consultants, external and internal, work on becoming increasingly highly leveraged. For consultants, the comparable step is to explain the approach to clients and gain their acceptance. Recognize that it takes two to tango. Highly leveraged consulting is

quite different from the conventional mode; both client and consultant have to understand how it works, and both have to be willing to do some experimenting to reap its substantial rewards.

2. *Select initial projects that have a high probability of success.* One key to encouraging managers to become willing participants in highly leveraged projects is to demonstrate to them that their people can actually achieve more than they've been achieving. In getting started, therefore, begin with projects that offer the maximum chance for success, projects where the client can be most certain of getting the most done with the least effort.

Often managers are not attuned to selecting sure-win projects. For example, I was exploring with a potential client which of several possible groups would be the best one to get started with on a project we were considering. She said, "Group X needs the most help. Why don't we start with them?" This is not an unusual managerial perspective, but the group that needs the most help is unlikely to be the one with the greatest chance of being successful—and success in the early steps of a project is critical. So you need to explain to your clients, as I did to this one, that after generating momentum with some other groups, she will have the experience and insights needed to make something happen with "group X."

One of the keys to achieving active participation from busy clients is to build in some of the zest factors mentioned in Chapter Three. To generate zest, the goals of consulting projects should be obviously important and provide a sense of urgency. Consider the projects mentioned earlier: MVE's order processing project concentrated on problems that were bothering people every day and costing the company money. The Morgan Bank project focused on providing timely service to dissatisfied customers. The State of Connecticut Department of Mental Retardation project aimed at eliminating the greatest source of fear and anxiety for employees and unnecessary expense for the state.

Projects like these, focused on urgent goals, quickly reveal the momentum the client's own people can generate and thus make clients more open to becoming involved in the consulting work. Suc-

cessful projects help overcome the rationalization that client employees don't have time to work on a project ("If we did, we wouldn't have
called in a consultant"). As in the Morgan Bank case, clients involved
in highly leveraged projects learn not only how to contribute to the
consulting project but also how to get more done in less time.

3. *Emphasize skill development in client personnel.* Except for
research projects or highly technical projects (where the consulting
arrangement may actually be more like outsourcing than management consulting), much of the work consultants traditionally perform in organizations can, with modest training, be done by clients'
own people, with some ongoing support from a consultant. Over
and over again I have seen client people at all levels and with all
sorts of backgrounds surprise their associates by demonstrating an
ability to learn these new techniques and apply them effectively.

In order to successfully have clients take over more project
responsibilities, both clients and consultants need to push past two
resistance points. The first of these is the deeply held faith in modern technology and its experts that we all tend to share. In con-
temporary society, the need to rely on experts is taken for granted.
When we have medical problems, we place ourselves under the care
of medical experts and expect that they will apply the best technology to the job of curing us. When we have to accomplish information and communications tasks, we turn ourselves over to the
computer and telecommunications experts. Throughout our lives,
we are trained to depend on the experts to give us the answers. In
business, consultants are the experts we depend on for "the right
answers." Conventional consulting methodologies reinforce this
perception by putting consultants in the lofty role of diagnosticians
and solution providers. This mystical faith in what the consultant's
magic potions can accomplish often motivates otherwise hard-
headed business executives to spend huge sums and considerable
time and energy on consulting projects that have no demonstrable
connection to bottom-line achievements.

The second point of resistance is the recurring issue of client
"busyness." Clients may resist investing the time required for

training and development. Indeed, the training may seem wasteful to some client managers. Since the consultants already know how to perform the work that must be done, managers may feel, "Why not let the consultants do what they are good at and let my busy people get on with their jobs?" To you client managers who feel this way, I urge you to consider this: if consultants had done the bulk of the work in the Morgan Bank, in the OSHA project, or in any of the other high-impact projects described in this book, they probably would not have accomplished as much as the people in the client organizations were able to accomplish. Worse, when the consultants completed their assignments, they would have walked away with valuable experience and insights that would no longer be available to the organization. Instead, in each high-impact project, clients participate actively and develop their own skills. The order entry people at MVE worked hard to learn process mapping and many related project management skills so they could provide the leadership in redesigning their processes. Henceforth, for the rest of their careers at MVE, they will be able to apply these skills and act with a new sense of confidence that they never would have developed as the mere recipients of consulting studies and recommendations.

4.   *Train internal consultants or facilitators to support the work.* When major change efforts are under way, the people who are trying to carry them out while keeping their regular job going at the same time can benefit from the support of a few facilitators who are concentrating on orchestrating the changes. This is a role that consultants can play while they are on the scene. When they leave, however, someone should take their place, and that's the job of internal facilitators.

The selection of some people in the client organization to serve as internal change facilitators supports the highly leveraged mode in a number of ways. First, these people can help ensure the success of the change effort, and they can multiply the client's return on its investment in consulting. They will be there after the consultants leave, able to apply their new skills indefinitely.

My own firm, dedicated as we are to highly leveraged consulting, very rarely begins an assignment without identifying internal consultants who will multiply our consulting effort and carry it forward after we leave. We provide training to these internal facilitators and work in a partnership mode with them to increase their learning.

5. *Develop an experimental, action-oriented mode of working.* The widely shared illusion that hiring a consultant is like buying an insurance policy—that the consultant will provide the "right answer" and prevent the client from heading down the wrong path—reinforces the one-big-solution, labor-intensive conventional paradigm. If the first project a consultant undertakes with a client is a study to determine the "right strategic directions" or some equally global concept, the client will wait a long time for the answer before they can get moving. Instead of developing implementation capability, the client sits and waits. If any really complex or difficult changes are recommended, and they usually are, they may be rejected as "impossible" or action may be delayed because "our people don't have the time for such an ambitious undertaking now." It is only after managers succeed with a number of rapid-cycle performance improvement and change projects that they develop the skill and confidence to successfully tackle very ambitious change projects.

So consultants who want to help their clients deal with large-scale, far-reaching strategic change efforts need to nurture and support those efforts with dozens of smaller-scale success experiences. These each need to be seen as an experiment in change. The experience gained from carrying out a number of such experiments provides the collective insight needed to manage larger-scale strategic changes.

6. *Work with the senior people who can most influence change and with large groups who can multiply the effort.* It is important to focus sufficient consulting time and attention on the few senior people who have major responsibility for producing the changes the consultant is helping to create. They are likely to have the most motivation for advancing the project, and they have more influence on stimulating others to move.

And, for the same reason, working with large numbers of people in structured workshops focused on organizing action to accomplish the needed changes is another means of mutliplying modest levels of consulting input into large-scale change. The experience of Dun & Bradstreet's Information Services Division illustrates how these multiplication strategies work.

Highly Leveraged Consulting at Dun & Bradstreet

In Chapter Six I outlined the launch of the quality effort at DBIS, which was led by Mike Berkin, the division's quality manager, with the help of consultants Douglas Smith and Charles Baum. It began with the selection of eight rapid-cycle projects, and as Mike Berkin describes it, proceeded as follows:

> Doug and Charlie were light-years different from the consultants I had worked with. They came on the scene, listened to us, and made us feel that they were on our side and were going to really try to help us. We did not want to invest further in training or anything else until we began to see results. We had seen over and over where people were trained and then did not accomplish anything.
>
> Charlie did the hands-on consulting, and Doug worked more on the strategic level. We started with the eight projects. We picked leaders with the help of Charlie and Doug to make sure these initial projects were designed for certain success.
>
> When we kicked off additional projects, I ran some of the launch workshops for the appointed project leaders, and Reuben Nyvelt, the training manager, ran a few. Charlie provided some coaching for us and sat in on some of these launch workshops.
>
> All the projects in the first wave were successful. All the additional projects were successful. When we launched the third wave, we began to do it in clusters. Reuben, Charlie, a few other people, and I went to Canada as a team, and we

launched a whole set of breakthroughs. In the morning we met with the leaders of all the projects, and then in the afternoon we had six simultaneous meetings, each facilitated by one of us. So by the end of the day, we had six breakthrough teams launched.

Charlie then created a workshop to train our facilitators. He ran some of those facilitator workshops with Reuben, provided him some support, and thereafter Reuben did the training of our facilitators. By the end of 1991 we had about twenty-five facilitators. And by that time Charlie was no longer involved with the work directly. Six months later, we had another seventy or eighty, for a total of over one hundred internal facilitators. Of the one hundred facilitators, some have done as many as twenty or thirty projects, others only four or five.

Charlie has come around occasionally for an informal review of our progress, and we chat on the phone every once in a while; but after the first few months of 1991, basically all of the work was taken over internally.

We have done about three thousand breakthrough projects, so we don't have to go through all the preliminaries anymore. When there is a problem or a goal or a thing we want to tackle, we bring the people together into a team, and everyone knows that the goal has to be clear, measurable and short-term.

By the end of 1993, all of the work to date was having an impact of about $30 million a year. By the end of 1994, there was $52 million worth of continuing and annualized impact from all the projects started since the beginning. These were in three categories: increased revenue generation, actual cost savings, and cost avoidance, by being able to produce more with the same expenses and resources.

In 1995 we began measuring only the impact of the current year's projects. In 1995 the incremental impact of the 1995 projects was $15 million a year, and that is a net figure—we subtracted all the expenses. That is on top of all the ongoing savings from previous years. And there may have been some additional projects, because not all got recorded.

When all of this started in 1991, we had four people in the quality shop. Today we are down to two.

Highly leveraged consulting? For an estimated $200,000 to $400,000 in outside consulting fees plus perhaps another few million dollars in internal consulting expenses, this division is enjoying a $60 or $70 million annual benefit. No one else I know has achieved quite this level, but every high-impact consulting project aims for this same sort of return on consulting resources.

Consultants who want to shift to a more highly leveraged approach have to abandon some of the comforting but counterproductive structures of the conventional mode. They will have to welcome and get comfortable with the participation of clients in the design and execution of their projects. And they will have to learn how to adjust the project pace to what seems right for the client.

Also, consultants, especially the less experienced ones, will have to develop strong interpersonal and change management coaching skills, skills they may not have focused on or been encouraged to develop. They will have to develop the skills to help their clients to think in new ways, to learn and grow. There must be a management development and organizational development component in what you do. For many consultants, this will require some new learning.

Finally, there are the economic issues: if yours is a large, traditional consulting firm and your economic health is rooted in large-scale, labor-intensive projects, you may anticipate adverse economic consequences from switching to high-impact consulting. That is not necessarily the case. There is one possible silver lining in the clouds: if the work that your large teams of consultants are doing is truly valuable to your clients, then there is no reason not to provide such help profitably. What these large groups of professionals are doing, however, might more likely be some sort of outsourced expert labor and not what I call management consulting. In fact, consulting firms might wish to consider identifying those individuals who are really management consultants and differentiating them from the larger pool of professionals who are really doing outsourced research or systems development work for the client.

Consultants may be required to do this as clients increasingly demand more demonstrable linkages between their investments in consulting and the benefits produced. It is my fervent desire that this book contribute to that market pressure.

Some Creative Highly Leveraged Work Designs

There are two keys to easing the path over the obstacles described in the previous paragraphs. One is to test the shift to highly leveraged consulting gradually. Client and consultant should select some first steps that appear achievable to both, steps they both agree they'd like to try. The second is to have some structured designs in mind. The next few paragraphs describe some pointers for designing highly leveraged consulting projects.

The GE "Workout" Model

John F. Welch, Jr., CEO of General Electric, recognized a paradox some years ago. After downsizing and reorganizing, the company had only 60 or 70 percent as many people as it had before. Yet, Welch discovered, his managers were trying to get their work done in the same old ways. He decided that GE needed to effect a massive shift to more effective work methods. In 1988 he commissioned a group of academics and consultants to help devise a method for accomplishing this goal. The result was the GE Workout process. With modest levels of consulting help, each GE business identified their key improvement requirements. Then, after some careful planning, they assembled a large group for a day or two to plan how the improvements were to be achieved. The ground rules required that the division's general managers attend the final session of the conference, listen to the group's conclusions and recommendations, and make on-the-spot decisions. Thus, with very modest levels of consulting input, thousands of GE people were able to contribute to modifying their work processes and accelerating the company's progress.[1]

The Workout approach is valuable not only with a single organization but also as a vehicle for interorganization collaboration. For example, consultants helped the senior managers of GE Lighting organize a meeting with the senior management of its largest customers, like General Motors. The aim was to improve the way they did business together, for the benefit of both businesses. With very modest consulting support, some major advances were made in intercompany partnership relations in these sessions.

The Workout methodology represents a design for highly leveraged consulting input. At General Reinsurance, the method was adapted to achieve widespread employee involvement in the company's quality and change processes. These sessions, called "quality action workshops," are supported by internal facilitators.

"Model Week" Projects

As described earlier, I have discovered that people are willing to shoot for amazingly challenging goals if they do not have to commit to meeting them indefinitely. That's what made it possible for United Aluminum's people to commit to and achieve 100 percent on-time delivery when they had, for years, struggled to get much beyond 80 percent. And that's what made it possible for the furnace superintendent and his team at Vitrine Products to agree to try to improve furnace efficiency by 7 percentage points although he had been certain that even 2 points was going to be a stretch.

Short-term, highly focused projects with a challenging goal often arouse a zestful "game" spirit. T-shirts or hats with slogans, martial music over the plant speaker system, senior managers visiting on the third shift—all add to the spirit of the endeavor. Once the participants have had the experience of reaching their "impossible" goal, often they have learned enough to sustain performance at the peak level or close to it. "Model week" projects are particularly appropriate with easily measurable improvements as the goal, such as speedier response to orders or customer requests, elimination of quality problems, and productivity improvement.

Pilot Projects

In many situations in which a conventional consultant would want to conduct a detailed study to assess whether some course of action was correct, a high-impact consultant might be more tempted to cut to the chase and say, "Let's try it and see how well it works." As described in Chapter Six, General Reinsurance selected six active customers and two prospects for pilot testing of its plan to implement customer service teams. At Vitrine Products, a pilot program was designed to test the performance improvement of one furnace before creating a process for increasing output from all the company's furnaces. In the automotive-parts plant example in Chapter Four, one of six production lines served as the pilot for a plantwide quality and delivery improvement project.

Breakthrough Projects

The "breakthrough strategy" is a discipline my firm developed for helping clients organize and sustain performance improvement. It is described in my book *The Breakthrough Strategy: Using Short-Term Successes to Build the High Performance Organization* and in many other articles and publications.

A breakthrough project is a rapid-cycle, results-focused project designed for client learning and well as achievement. Many of the rapid-cycle projects described earlier in this book were breakthrough projects. There are three key ingredients to a breakthrough project:

1. *Measurable client results*. Reducing patient-caused injuries at Fairfield Hills Hospital, increasing the number of eucalyptus logs loaded on each railway car in South Africa, reducing "opacity" incidents in Consolidated Edison's package boilers, getting Motorola's new products to market in ninety days—these goals, all easily measurable targets, had to be achieved in "rapid-cycle" time, without sacrificing any other activities under way in the organization.

2. *Client learning and development*. Clients learn how to select and organize a results-focused project, to mobilize the involvement of the right people, to lay out a practical work plan, and to coordinate all of the steps needed to achieve their goal. After each breakthrough project, clients should be much more qualified to carry out the next one.

3. *Testing of consultant-provided insights, tools, and techniques*. Consultants introduce their ideas, concepts, and tools during the breakthrough project so that clients have a chance to see how they work before making a big commitment.

Almost every large-scale change or improvement challenge can be attacked via incremental breakthrough projects that deliver immediate payoffs for the client, develop client capability, and test the consultant's inputs.

Simple Concepts, Profound Differences

In Chapters Four through Eight I have outlined how clients and consultants can shift from long-cycle-time, labor-intensive, high-risk conventional consulting to high-impact consulting. These chapters have described how to reverse the five frequently fatal flaws of conventional consulting and transform them into high-return contributors. As clients and consultants make these shifts, they will radically alter the way they work together and multiply by many times the returns on clients' consulting investment.

In order to move effectively into a mode in which clients and consultants share responsibility for producing results, the parties will have to work out their project agreements (that is, their contracts) more carefully and deliberately. Consultants will have to pay more heed to the way senior client managers convey performance improvement requirements to their people. And, finally, clients and consultants will have to learn to overcome their anxiety-produced defense mechanisms and communicate much more effectively.

The next few chapters describe how these shifts in their working relationship can support high-impact consulting, with highly leveraged results. The shifts will contribute not only to making consulting much more effective but also to making it much more fun and personally rewarding.

PART THREE

Creating High-Impact Partnerships

9

Create a Contract for Collaboration Instead of a Proposal for a Job

Many changes were under way simultaneously in this very successful financial services company. The company was introducing new products and new ways of serving its customers. Management was realigning the marketing division, and the groups that supported the marketing function would have to change their way of doing business. As all these changes were being planned and coordinated, several senior managers suddenly realized that no "home" had been established for several staff functions that served the marketing division. Moreover, the new marketing unit would need a number of additional services that had not yet been spelled out or included in the new structure.

A consulting firm was already at work supporting many of the changes under way in the company, so it was natural to ask them to look into these unresolved issues. They were asked to investigate whether a new department might be established to encompass both the as-yet-unassigned groups as well as the new functions that were going to be needed. There was some logic to the idea, since the functions were all somewhat related. There were a few informal conversations, and then the consultants prepared a brief proposal outlining what they would do. Since the project seemed to be such a straightforward one compared with the other complex changes under

147

way, management read and approved the proposal rather quickly. Then the consultants went to work.

The consultants interviewed a number of people in the company. They did research on how similar functions were organized and operated in other companies. They deliberated among themselves about what might be a serviceable structure that would meet the client's requirements. Finally, they developed a comprehensive set of recommendations for establishing a new staff department.

When the consultants presented their findings and recommendations, everyone was impressed with the quality of the work and the consultants' insights and perspectives. But very little of the report was acted on, because it did not align with a number of decisions that had already been made before the project was launched. So the consulting effort, while causing no harm, contributed little or nothing to the client.

This case illustrates how consulting projects are often launched. When a senior management group believes that consulting might help them, they give a consulting team a description of their needs, answer the consultants' questions, and then wait for them to present a proposal outlining how they will meet those needs. These proposals, like the one in this case, are typically composed by the consultants and describe the work they will do. When clients receive the proposal, they either approve it or turn it down. The consultants write the proposal on their own, because they and their client view consulting as a set of tasks carried out by consultants on behalf of their client instead of a collaboration between them, as advocated in this book. The whole process is generally carried out in a back-and-forth, hand-off fashion, even where there is a close working relationship (as there was in this case).

Here the consultants saw their job as devising the best solution possible, a purely intellectual task rather than a collaborative project. They did not stop to test readiness as described in Chapter Five. Moreover, they did not pause to observe that the people who would have a role in making the final decisions, busy as they were with dozens of other issues, had not really discussed with each other their respective views on this project. A few questions would have revealed that on some of these issues, irreversible decisions had already been made. On other issues there was no consensus. Some readiness questions and "What if?" testing of possible conclusions would have revealed that there were resource and organizational relationship constraints that any solution would have to adhere to. So it was quite naive for the consultants to prepare a proposal and assume that a go-ahead from the client would mean likely support for the project's recommendations. The process failed to encourage a collaborative examination of the best way to carry out the project so as to ensure its success.

Moreover, the willingness of consultants to accept responsibility for preparing proposals, as in this case, allows the client to disengage and assume little or no responsibility for shaping the project, thus putting the client in a passive role from the start.

These are the kinds of weaknesses that characterize the typical consultant-designed proposal, which in most conventional consulting serves as the instrument for defining and launching a consulting project.

Collaborative Contracts, Not One-Way Proposals

Implementing a high-impact consulting project, by contrast, requires the client and consultant to thoughtfully explore what they want to achieve together and how to achieve it. As they reach agreements, they jointly document those agreements. The result of this process is the *project contract*. This is a carefully prepared written statement outlining both parties' roles and commitments in their joint undertaking, from the beginning of the project to the end. If only the most immediate steps can be specified when the contract is created, provision is made for the parties to review their progress and create a more detailed plan for subsequent stages.

The fundamental consideration in creating a contract should be how well the client and consulting team can work together to accomplish results, not how competent the consultants are in any given technical area. If the client takes the conventional stance of a customer purchasing analytical services from a vendor, it will be more difficult to create a meaningful dialogue on issues like client readiness. Only in a true partnership can the parties identify potential low-risk, rapid-cycle projects.

Instead of rushing off to prepare a proposal, the consultant to the financial services company described above should have asked a few of the client's people for their ideas about the best solution. They then might have gathered, if only briefly, some of the key players to gauge their understanding of what they wanted from the consulting project and what sort of solutions might be acceptable. They might have made notes of what they heard in these discussions and circulated the notes back to the client's managers as a draft "contract" for the project. If there were still some open issues, those would be the agenda for continuing discussion. If there were any conflicts within management, they would need to be identified and the project designed to deal with them. This is the contracting process.

Creating a Partnership, Not Buying and Selling

Contracting in this mode reflects a partnership more than a buyer-vendor interaction. Although the client is certainly the "buyer" and the consultant the "vendor," they do not conduct their initial exploration as if they were negotiating a sale. The buy-sell mode can work if the consultant is selling a package of technical work or other outsourced services. If, however, the aim is to create a working partnership among people who will be jointly accountable for significant client results, then a typical buy-sell "negotiation" will not accomplish that end.

In high-impact consulting, in fact, the contracting process is as important as the contract itself. It consists of a structured approach to managing all of the issues detailed in the previous chapters: identifying the most urgent client goals, assessing client readiness, defining specific goals for the first subprojects, and agreeing on the best way for the client and consultant to work together on the project.

I am not suggesting that clients shouldn't "shop around" in hiring a consultant. When a client is uncertain about which consultant to hire, an initial screening can be performed by requesting an informal introductory memorandum from potential consultants; this serves as a get-acquainted step. Once the client managers have narrowed the field to a few consultants, however, they should shift modes and pursue the process described in this chapter with all of the candidates. In that way, the shopping around process will permit the right kind of dialogue to take place, and it will give client and consultant a chance to engage in some healthy interaction and exploration. The key is to break out of the arms-length interaction that often characterizes competitive bidding and requests for proposals, in which consulting projects are treated as commodities to be purchased rather than as joint efforts to produce results.

Identify *the* Client

Perhaps it seems odd to make the point now, since I have made so many general references to "the client," but one early and critical step in the contracting process is to specify who *the* client really is. *The* client is the one person (or explicitly defined group) who accepts personal accountability for seeing to it that the client organization makes use of and benefits from the consulting help.

In the financial services case, several senior managers had raised organizational issues in conversations with the consultants. The consultants mentioned to those people that perhaps it was something they might offer help in resolving. There was general agreement, and the proposal followed. But there was no effort to specify one person who would be accountable for working with the consultant team to ensure a successful outcome. The need to identify *the* client is frequently overlooked in launching a consulting project. As in the financial services case, projects are launched because a number of managers believe that "something needs to be done," and the consultants offer to do it. But when their recommendations are presented, there is no one person clearly designated to receive them and make sure they are dealt with.

Here are two vignettes that highlight the difference between identifying *the* client and failing to do so:

> Mary McKreath is senior vice president of engineering for a telecommunications equipment company. Her company's CEO and its executive committee have agreed that their corporate strategic planning unit should study the rapid shifts occurring in the company's customer base. The issue is whether the company should reorganize its businesses to respond to these shifts.

Scenario 1

McKreath, as a member of the committee, attends the meetings when the study plan is discussed and participates actively. She reads and comments on the consulting group's proposal. Once the proposal is approved and the strategic planning unit gets to work, McKreath, along with all the other members of the executive committee, turns back to her very demanding job.

Scenario 2

As in Scenario 1, the executive committee agrees to the study. But the CEO also announces that he has asked Mary McKreath to take responsibility for the project. Her mission will be to work with the strategic planning unit to guide their work and make certain they do the best job possible. Once the plan is accepted, the CEO adds, McKreath will be spearheading the implementation process.

Scenario 1 could easily lead to a situation in which everyone supports the consultant's findings but no one takes responsibility for ensuring an effective response. In Scenario 2, McKreath is clearly *the* client for the work to be done by the strategic planning unit. One can be certain she will be thinking about implementation possibilities well before the end of the project.

It is much easier, incidentally, for internal consultants than for external consultants to drift into projects where there is no clearly identified client because their fees usually do not have to be negotiated. So when they are in a meeting and a senior manager says, "We ought to look into . . ." or "Would it be possible for someone to find out how much demand there would be if . . ." an internal consultant, eager to contribute, may take that as an assignment and crank up a project without defining a client or creating a contract.

We have seen many corporate staff consulting projects that got started because there was a shared conviction by some senior managers that "something needs to be done about . . ." and that conviction was conveyed to internal consultants. In response, the internal group launched its efforts, overlooking the fact that no one was accountable for the project. Thus there was no one to play the partner role with the consultants nor to make sure that the consultants' work was translated into bottom-line results. I have seen such projects go on for years and rack up huge expenditures, with the internal consultants fruitlessly trying to "sell" senior people on doing something about their recommendations and the senior people all agreeing that "something really should be done."

No matter how many other people are involved in exploring and conducting the project, it is *the* client who, from the first moment, is the consultant's counterpart within the organization. (This point was touched on in the section on mapping in Chapter Five.) It is *the* client who makes a clear commitment to being accountable, with the consultant, for achieving the specified results.

Create the Contract

Once *the* client is defined, that person or group and the consultants need to work jointly on creating the contract. Here are some guidelines you might follow in creating a project contract:

1. *Frame the goals of the project.* What are the overall aims of the project? How should the project contribute to the organization's progress? How does it relate to the organization's strategies and the other important activities going on? In other words, the project should not be viewed as an isolated endeavor but as an element of and contributor to overall progress. The contract should specify how the project relates to other efforts going on in the organization.

The parties need to answer the following questions. What are the longer-range goals to which the project is contributing (reducing costs, speeding turnaround time, meeting customer needs, serving new markets)? Are there by-product outcomes that are important in creating momentum for ongoing progress? Are there some specific client development and training goals? Are there any organizational structure issues? Are there culture change goals? How must the project be designed both to meet its immediate aims and to create a foundation for future progress?

In addition to the explicit goals of the project, there are often unwritten expectations that need to be smoked out. Any discussion of project goals must recognize the occasional desire, conscious or unconscious, of clients to have consultants not only get a job done but also to make them look good, eliminate a competitor, or advance a pet project. These types of motivations are subtly woven into the fretwork of project decision making. The careful construction of a mutual contract will make it more likely that such hidden issues will be identified and dealt with in ways that do minimum harm to project goals.

2. *Specify some rapid-cycle projects.* From the array of broad project goals, client and consultant should identify one or several rapid-cycle subprojects. These are the kinds of breakthrough projects that were described in Chapter Six. The goals of these projects have to be discussed and negotiated not only between *the* client and consultant but also with the people in the client organization who will be responsible for achieving results.

In identifying the first few project goals, client readiness assessment needs to play a key role. Initial projects need to be selected on the basis of what is learned about what the client might be ready, willing, and able to do.

Along with definitions of the project's tangible goals, there should be some clear statements of how the results are to be measured. It is important for the contract to detail not only the first rapid-cycle projects but also to sketch out the possible sequencing of next-step projects.

It also bears repeating that each of these rapid-cycle projects differs from the "phases" of a conventional consulting project: there may be a long sequence of phases in such a project, but there is no promise of any real results until all the phases have been carried out and the entire project has been completed. Rapid-cycle, high-impact consulting projects, whether they aim at large or small goals, are designed to produce some tangible results quickly.

3. *Define project roles and resource contributions.* The contract should describe the contributions of the various parties. What are the unique "expert" contributions the consultant will make? Will it be study and interpretation? Will it be ideas for major shifts in strategy? What will client people be expected to contribute? How will the consultant's expertise and know-how be blended with know-how in the client organization? How much time and energy is each party going to invest? In addition to the main players, what support will be required from other units inside or outside the organization, and how will that support be engaged?

4. *Lay out a project work plan and methodology.* The parties need to create a tentative work plan outlining how the project might be carried out and how the clients and consultants will work together. The work plan should include the complete cast of characters (from the client mapping) and descriptions of the roles of each group and each person.

The plan should also include a work schedule outlining the steps of the project, who will be involved in each step, and how it will be carried out. The work plan should cover all of the steps up to the point when the initial results should have been achieved. Key milestones along the way should be identified, and the progress that should have been achieved by each mile-stone detailed.

In laying out the work plan, the parties must ask the following questions. How will the project be directed? How will the various interested parties in the client organization be wired into the project? How often will progress reviews be conducted? how? by whom? If the senior people who are contracting for the project are not to be actively involved in it, how will they be kept informed and involved? If fresh insights are developed during the project and it appears that a change in direction should be considered, who will be responsible for raising the issue? How should such changes be accomplished?

To accomplish its goals, the contracting exploration must encourage real give-and-take between the parties. To facilitate open discussion, both consultant and client should do some homework before meeting. They should be prepared to walk through the elements covered in the above outline, discussing each one, testing possible ways to move, test-ing the connection between some possible rapid-cycle projects and longer-term goals. This kind of discussion tends to break down peo-ple's expectations for a stereotypical customer-vendor relationship.

Contracting for high-impact consulting is an iterative process. At end of each exploratory meeting, someone should be responsi-ble for summarizing the conclusions of the meeting in the form of a draft outline of project goals and activities. Sometimes this person will be the consultant. Sometimes one or two members of both the consulting and client teams can be given the job to record the con-sensus. The product of this work will be the beginnings of the pro-ject contract. The principal client leaders and the consulting team need to meet to review the draft, assess it against their expectations, and discuss how to strengthen it.

Sometimes clients complain that this exploratory process will take too much time. But usually this kind exploration can be done rather quickly. And even if it does take a bit longer than just having the consultant do a proposal—as it certainly would have in the case that opened the chapter—it won't be nearly as wasteful as doing the wrong project.

Versatility: A Key Ingredient of the Contracting Process

In shaping a high-impact contract, in order to design the project so that it aligns well with what is being discovered about the client's readiness issues, the consultant must be very flexible and responsive. This is not an easy task for many consulting groups and individual consultants, who have favorite methodologies that they employ to deal with certain kinds of situations. With a solution or an approach already in mind, the consultant may fall into the trap of trying to fit the problem to the method, as illustrated by the following anecdote:

> A graying, slightly portly gentleman entered the "Smith & Company Formal Wear" emporium. He explained to Mr. Smith that he had been invited to a black tie dinner celebrating his employer's silver wedding anniversary. "Would you have a size 46 tuxedo for me to use next Saturday?" he asked. Smith had just finished outfitting the principals of a wedding that was to take place on the same day, and several of them were the same size as this customer. He realized instantly that the only suit available in size 46 was a powder-blue suit with wide satin lapels, which had last been worn to a high school prom by the football team captain.

I ask participants in my consultant training seminars to guess what Smith says at that moment. They laugh and offer possibilities like these: "Sir, you look like someone who would never want to dress in the same dull way as everyone else" or "Wow, would you look fantastic in blue! Let me see if I have something in blue." Since I tell this anecdote just after discussing the importance of testing client readiness, I challenge the seminar participants with this: "Isn't it important for Smith to test his customer's readiness, that is, his wishes and desires?" They respond: "No way! Smith is going to push the baby-blue number with the satin lapels."

The moral of the story is this: if you have only one suit to rent, that's the suit you are going to push. If you have only one consulting solution in mind, that's the solution you are going to recommend. Consultants who become too locked in to their standard approaches are as inflexible and nonresponsive as our formalwear salesman. In fact, when consultants speak about the importance of being well prepared for client meetings, they usually mean that they should have a clear point of view and be prepared to explain and defend it no matter what objections the client raises. There is probably not one consultant in a hundred who would be willing to go to a restaurant that had no menu, where the proprietor simply tells you what is the best food to eat. But many consultants think nothing of offering their clients the single best solution and fail to offer them any other choices.

Versatility is the alternative. Versatility encourages consultants to make available to their clients the same power that all of us want in our role as consumers of products and services: choice! To provide a menu with choices, however, means having a variety of options ready to respond to a client's questions or requests. With a range of options, the parties can review the possibilities, discuss them, and speculate about how each would work. Gradually they can converge on a jointly created and mutually agreed upon contract.

Such an exploration leads to a sense of joint ownership of the direction selected. So clearly, in order to make use of what they learn about client readiness, it is necessary for consultants to develop "design versatility," which is the capacity to provide a menu of project possibilities that can be shaped to match unique client readiness.

Trapped by Right Answers

An almost insurmountable barrier to versatility exploration is the entrapment of consultants by their views of the "right answers." In any new situation, when a potential client describes his or her situation it is fairly common for the consultant to develop a sense of how the consulting project should be designed and what the solution might look like. And once this conviction takes shape, the consultants do less listening and more selling. This digging-in of heels is even more exaggerated when the consultant senses that he has a somewhat different perspective on the situation than the client and that the client, in fact, may not even grasp the issues properly. Rigidity is worst when the potential clients begin to express what they want the consultants to do and the consultants feel they are being asked to do the wrong assignment.

Just as soon as consultants sense these gaps in viewpoint emerging, their anxiety begins to rise. They become preoccupied with not becoming trapped into acting on the wrong assumptions or accepting the wrong assignment. At that moment, their listening mechanisms shut down. How often does this happen? Very often. Remember, clients and consultants always view the situation somewhat differently. Those differences can make the relationship productive, or it can lead to a freeze-up. Consider this case, which I have used in seminars with many hundreds of consultants:

Electron Digital is a distribution company that handles a variety of electronic control equipment for manufacturing and other automation uses. The president was recruited into the company a few years ago, and since that time performance has stagnated. The president calls on a consulting firm to see if they can provide some help.

At the first meeting with a partner from the firm, the president comes to the point quickly. He feels the key is to accelerate sales volume. He admits that the company has a number of other problems that need to be dealt with, but he wants the consultant to focus on improving the performance of the sales force first. Since the salespeople seem to lack many basic skills, the president's first priority is for the consultant to design and conduct training for the sales force. Once this is under way, the president says, the consultant can also begin looking at the incentive compensation plan and related issues. How does the consultant feel about taking on this assignment?

Now the moment of truth has arrived. The consultant's review of the briefing materials, her cursory research before the visit, and even the little that the president has said in this meeting all suggest that this company has many problems that cannot be cured by sales training. The company's prices seem to be high. Their distribution methods are inefficient. They have had some quality problems. One of the consultant's informants told her that the company's technical support group is very weak.

So what should the consultant do? Pause for a moment and consider this question. I have seen hundreds of consultants role-play this case, and 95 percent of them became preoccupied with not accepting the wrong assignment. They felt they would be doing the client a disservice by conducting a big training program that would not solve the company's problems. In role-playing this case, almost every consultant stops listening to the client early in the interview and concentrates on subtly (or not so subtly) maneuvering the client away from his desire for training. In almost every case this maneuvering irritates the CEO. But even if the consultants are aware they are frustrating the president, they insist that ethical considerations require them to confront the president with the "real" issues and not be trapped into doing a training program. Both experienced and inexperienced consultants fall into the same pattern. Within a few minutes of meeting a CEO for the first time, they are challenging the CEO's judgment and urging him to abandon his convictions and substitute a different approach.

The trap that snares most consultants in dealing with such situations is that they quickly form a mental image of what the client means by whatever he is asking for (in this case, "training"). Once this image is formed, they leap to conclusions, as if their hastily formed, untested image were a fact. Then, uneasy about being stuck with the wrong assignment, they forget everything they ever heard about testing readiness. Instead, they begin sparring with the client at the very moment when they should be trying to understand the client's viewpoints and developing a good working relationship.

I ask seminar participants who are adamant that a training program would be the wrong solution to describe exactly what the CEO meant when he used the word *training*. What sort of interventions did he mean to include? Which did he mean to exclude? It doesn't take them long to admit that the CEO didn't say much about it, and since they did not probe into the president's views, they really have very little idea what he meant. This is par for the course: as soon as consultants feel a bit uncomfortable with where they think a client may be heading, they try to maneuver the discussion in another direction. That is a poor strategy for developing a real understanding of the client's views.

When otherwise qualified consultants fail to establish rapport with a new client, it is often because the clients perceive the consultants as trying to straighten them out. No wonder that the client may become somewhat resentful. And no wonder that such discussions may unnerve the client and lead to a confrontation or even to the decision to not proceed with the project: "It sounds good, Ms. Consultant, but I'm beginning to think that we shouldn't take this on right at the moment. We'll give you a call." When this happens, the consultant may rationalize, "Well, I'd rather not get the job than do the wrong assignment." But that is a false choice.

Designing with Versatility

By employing design versatility, a consultant can avoid many of these obstacles to a good exploration. The consultant needs to have a menu of possible project approaches. Then, keeping his or her anxiety at bay and probing for the reasons that a client is asking for something in a certain way, the consultant can begin to identify what the client really wants. And then, at an appropriate time, the consultant can present some of the choices on the consulting "menu." As these are explored with the client, the consultant will gain deeper understanding of what might work. And with this understanding, the consultant can begin to fashion a "common ground" project design—that is, a project that is a good match with what the client wants to do and also makes sense to the consultant. The Electron Digital case illustrates how it works.

After discussing the concept of design versatility and the idea of presenting a menu of project possibilities, I ask the seminar participants who have been arguing with the CEO whether they can imagine even one possible "common ground" first step project that they would undertake with Electron Digital. Such a project would have to meet two requirements:

1. It would accept, at least for the moment, the CEO's belief that "sales force training" is what should be done.
2. It would have to be a sensible step for the consultants.

At first this seems impossible to many in the group. Then one person makes a suggestion like this: "How about if we were to suggest interviewing the managers in one or two branches about what they think are the differences between their top-performing salespeople and their poorest salespeople? We could then come back and discuss the findings with the CEO and discuss some tentative next steps." Everyone agrees that step could provide some useful insight and permit further dialogue with the CEO. Then I ask the group for another illustration, and then another, and then I ask everyone to think of four or five such projects. Not everyone can come up with that many, but most consultant groups can develop a list of twenty or thirty possibilities. You might try it yourself; then consult Exhibit 9.1, which lists a number of the versatility ideas various consultants have suggested.

At this point, I summarize the lessons of the case. First, no consultant should show up in a new situation and try to straighten out the client in the first few minutes. Second, consultants need not go into battle formation as soon as they find themselves in disagreement with a client. Even if they do not confront a client

EXHIBIT 9.1. Possible Get-Started Projects for Electron Digital.

The following are potential common-ground projects that are not inconsistent with the client's view that training is the way to go but also appear, from the consultant's vantage point, to be a sensible first step. They have been grouped under two categories, fact-finding steps and experimenting and pilot-testing projects.

A. **Fact-Finding Steps**
- Interview some sales managers and/or salespeople about what they think makes for successful selling in the company.
- Interview the best salespeople to find out what skills or actions they consider to be keys to their success.
- Interview some customers (of Electron Digital and of its competitors) to find out what the major influences are on their buying decisions. What role does the salesperson's performance play in their buying decisions?
- Spend some time in one or two branches, chatting with managers and salespeople about what they think are the keys to success and what would be required to increase sales volume.
- Conduct a formal companywide survey of current sales practices.
- Review sales results across regions to identify differences between better and poorer performers.
- Review the current or most recent programs used to train salespeople, and assess their impact on sales results.
- Assess the sales practices of successful competitors, and compare them with Electron Digital's practices.

B. **Experimenting and Pilot-Testing Projects**
- Select one or two pilot branches and conduct an experiment with the managers of those branches for a few weeks. Let them try out a few ideas about what they could do to improve sales, and then see if these ideas work.
- Similarly, collaborate with the sales managers in one or two branches on working with salespeople on a sales performance improvement effort.
- Work with a small pilot group of supervisors. Meet with them periodically over a month or two. Have them each create and then try out his or her own experiment in improving sales in the branches. At each session, review progress and identify what is and what isn't working.
- Coach supervisors to work more effectively with a subset of their salespeople.
- Focus on one branch or region, and provide whatever support and training is needed to increase its sales performance.

(or potential client) at once with what they think is wrong about what the client is saying, it doesn't mean they are automatically accepting everything the client says or that they will do exactly what the client is asking for. They are merely avoiding confrontation and permitting the exploration to move forward constructively and openly.

Client and consultant should aim at identifying a few modest next steps that make sense to both of them. They may do no more than sketch the outlines of longer-term goals, since it may be necessary to create a solid foundation before attacking those goals. For many consultants, this shift will be difficult: they need to abandon the notion that their immediate goal is to design a one-year project involving a large team of consultants that can begin moving in next Monday. Instead, their aim will be to offer a menu of first-step projects and narrow them down to a few sure winners.

After I review these "lessons" with seminar participants, and keeping the long menu of possible common-ground projects in mind, I ask seminar participants to try the role-play interviews again with their Electron Digital "CEOs." In these follow-up role plays, the consultants no longer need to maneuver the client to abandon his position, and they become much better listeners. In virtually every case, offering a menu of a few possible first-step projects gets the interview moving out of a selling mode and into a collaboration mode. When the client asks the consultant, "How might you approach a task like this?" the consultant can respond, "I have a few thoughts about how this project might get started. Let me share them, and then you can give me your thoughts, and we can see whether there are others we can think of."

As consultants become more flexible in designing projects, they will find that it becomes easier to think of many project design variations when confronted with a client's statement of need. The greater the number of variations that consultants have in mind, the more likely that the chosen path will respond to client readiness and be loaded for success.

When first experimenting with versatility, consultants may have difficulty breaking free of their old patterns. It will take some practice to develop the spontaneity and flexibility needed to devise a variety of approaches to any given client situation. Client managers should also do some versatility preparation. What are some of the different ways you believe consultants might be able to attack the challenge you are trying to deal with? What are the advantages and limitations of each? If both client and consultant have a range of options in mind, then they can lay a foundation for a highly creative exploration.

In order to make this approach work and to be ready to offer a menu of choices to clients, consultants need to do some homework before their meetings. Telephone interviewing can be the enabler on this.

Telephone Interviewing

Since consultants are very preoccupied when they are actually in a meeting with a client, they can't possibly do much thinking about versatility. It is useful, therefore, if the consultant brings a few versatility ideas to the meeting. That means doing some creative brainstorming before arriving at the client meeting. In order to do it in advance, however, the consultant needs to find out enough about the situation. The key to being able to do this is to conduct a premeeting telephone interview. Ordinarily, the client describes in a telephone call what he or she has in mind, in the most general terms. Then an appointment is set for a meeting.

Consultants should learn how to get more information on the telephone while they are setting up a client meeting. Once a date has been set with a client, the consultant should avoid ending the conversation with, "Fine, I'll see you Thursday morning." Instead, he or she should add, "If you have a moment, maybe you could say just a bit more about what our agenda will be so that I can do some thinking in advance and be certain to bring along any papers that might be useful."

That question often encourages the client to provide further insight into his or her thinking, which permits both parties to do some more detailed preparation, including the development of a menu of action possibilities. The key to applying these ideas in meetings with clients (and potential clients) is to make it a rule never to go to a client interview (especially with potential new clients) without a "menu" of possible project ideas.

Use some advance telephone interviewing, and brainstorm your versatility ideas in advance with a colleague, if that is possible. If it is not, at least put down on a pad as many ideas as you can think of. You may or may not use any one of these, but they'll give you the confidence that if you listen carefully to the client and find out what he or she is really ready, willing, and able to do, you'll surely be able to come up with a few possibilities that will satisfy both of you.

Clients should always feel cheated when a consultant presents only one approach. Usually that means that they are getting "the standard product." Clients should insist on hearing a range of options from a consultant and having the pluses and minuses of each option explored and discussed. Why did the consultants recommend what they recommended? What were the alternatives considered, and why were they rejected by the consultant?

With some open back-and-forth dialogue, careful listening by the consultant, and the consideration of a variety of possible get-started projects, client and consultant will piece together the contract for their joint project. In contracting this way, they move into a partnership mode from the first moment. The contract they develop is not merely a job description for the consultant, but a joint pledge by both parties to produce some measurable results.

10

Help Senior Managers Demand Better Results—and Get Them

A partner in a well-known consulting firm was asked by a vice president of manufacturing at an electronics company to visit a recently acquired plant. The consultant was told that the plant was a poor performer that needed help in many areas, including productivity, inventory control, employee relations, and quality. When the consultant asked what had been communicated to the plant manager about his impending visit, the vice president replied that he had sent the plant manager a memorandum advising him that the consultants would be coming. It asked that the plant management cooperate, and it assured the plant people that the consultant's fees would be paid as a corporate expense.

When the consultant arrived on the scene, with several colleagues, the plant manager and his principal associates readily admitted that theirs was a poor-performing plant. "And why wouldn't it be?" they asked, explaining over the course of several hours how corporate management had prevented them from improving their performance. They were allocated no funds to replace inadequate equipment. The most difficult to manufacture products were assigned to their plant, while the other plants received easier tasks. They had been forced to cut people whose services were needed. And corporate staff was constantly pulling their people off the job for safety training, quality training, leadership training, and other corporate programs that were not directly related to getting the job done.

When the consultants described their mission, the plant people groaned and insisted that trying to improve the plant without capital and other corporate support would be futile. The consultants said they would convey those feelings to senior management, but in the meantime they would carry out a number of studies. Whenever they invited the plant manager or other plant people to collaborate with them in an action step, however, it was always the wrong time, or something else had to be done first, or there was "no sense doing it until corporate management loosened up the purse strings."

Many months went by, and the consultants sent a variety of recommendations for improvement to the plant managers and the vice president of manufacturing, but very little progress was achieved. Eventually the consultants departed.

Unfortunately, this scenario is all too common. A consultant's study reveals many opportunities for improvement, but no improvement takes place, because the people who have to take action are not sufficiently motivated. This chapter shows how conventional consulting patterns frequently trap consultants into working with clients who don't have a strong drive to make a consulting project succeed. The traditional process, by its nature, offers an escape hatch to senior managers who should be communicating strong expectations to the people who need to be motivated. This chapter describes how high-impact consulting, by contrast, encourages senior managers to communicate clear performance expectations.

Hiring a Consultant Cannot Substitute for Making Demands

What consultant has not been thwarted by a chain of events exactly like those described above? A top-level manager, determined to achieve significant performance improvement, engages a consultant to help. This senior executive describes the challenge and outlines the goals. Once the deal is struck, the consultant, assignment in hand, heads out to work with the lower-level "implementing clients." When she arrives, however, she discovers that they have little or no motivation to accomplish the results she has been hired to help them accomplish. This forces the consultant to choose from three bad options: complaining to the boss about the indifference of the subordinates, ignoring implementation issues, or becoming a missionary and trying to persuade people to implement her recommendations.

In the case described above, the vice president of manufacturing instructed the plant manager to welcome the consultants and cooperate with them, and that's exactly what the plant manager did. He and his associates were very open and hospitable. What the vice president had failed to do was convey to the plant's management that they were required to improve the performance of the plant by certain specific amounts. Like many senior managers who hire consultants, the vice president was hoping that the project, if done well, would produce the results. That unrealistic hope allowed him to sidestep the emotional strain of demanding that the plant managers meet higher standards.

The defect lies in a pattern of intraorganizational communication that is all too common when a consultant is involved. Exhibit 10.1 portrays how the strongly motivated "power client" conveys the improvement requirement to the consultant but fails to convey it to the implementing clients. Consequently, highly motivated consultants are placed in the position of trying to get the job done with less-than-enthusiastic or even resentful working-level clients.

Consider the following assignments, which almost any management consultant would have been delighted to receive:

INVENTORY CONTROL

The president of a multidivisional corporation told the director of its technical services department, an internal consulting group, that control over rising inventory and a significant

EXHIBIT 10.1. Misdirected Demands.

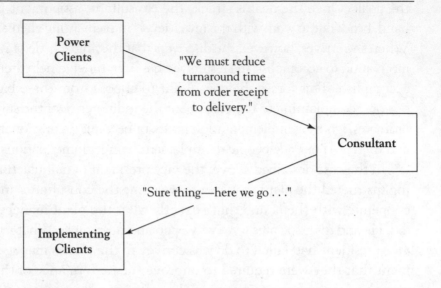

increase in inventory turns were two of the corporation's most important goals. The director was charged with taking steps to achieve some significant gains in the following year and to bring overall inventory growth under control.

ADMINISTRATIVE PRODUCTIVITY

A consulting firm was invited by the CEO of a health maintenance organization to help "reengineer" its operations to increase productivity and improve service to subscribers. The consultants were given carte blanche to proceed, and department heads throughout the operation were instructed to give their complete support to the effort.

In both of these cases, an executive with the necessary power and position gave a challenging assignment to a consultant. Both assignments addressed important client goals and were broad in scope and concept, and in each case the key executive indicated a real commitment to cooperate with and support the consultant. But what happened when the consultants went forth to accomplish the mission?

INVENTORY CONTROL

When the consultants began to move into the corporation's divisions and manufacturing plants to work on inventory control, they encountered a mixed reaction. Several divisions pointed to inventory control programs that were already under way. Others said that reduced inventories would mean reduced service. Since this occurred during an economic downturn, some divisions implied that keeping their business afloat took precedence over controlling their inventory. There was relatively little interest in working on the goals the consulting group had been charged with achieving.

ADMINISTRATIVE PRODUCTIVITY

The consulting team introduced a new work flow design and dozens of sound scheduling and control programs in several of the largest departments. There was, however, little noticeable effect on productivity, quality, or service.

Because the success of consulting projects depends so heavily on the way performance expectations are conveyed (or not conveyed) to the implementing clients, both senior managers and the consultants they hire need to take a much more penetrating look at these issues than either usually does.

Management's Toughest Task

Over twenty years ago I wrote, "Few managers possess the capacity— or feel compelled—to establish high performance-improvement expectations in ways that elicit results. Indeed, the capacity for such demand making could be the most universally underdeveloped management skill."[1] All of my observations since then have confirmed this conviction. Every year, a profusion of organizational improvement tools and techniques are adopted by thousands of organizations as hoped-for magic cures. Yet the single most critical difference between high-performing, fast-moving organizations and their less successful counterparts remains the same. It is the capacity (and resolve) of the senior executive to convey to his or her associates that much better results will be required, and to convey that message convincingly.

Expectations Profoundly Affect Performance

The differences between excellent demand making and weak demand making are very clear to management observers. Everyone with an interest in organizational performance has been impressed by the impact John Welch's demand making has had on General Electric. When he told his business heads that they would have to be number 1 or 2 in their sector or they would be replaced or have their business sold, there was little doubt in the minds of these executives that they had to respond. Most did respond, and rather successfully. When GE vice chairman Lawrence Bossidy became CEO of AlliedSignal in the early nineties, he too issued some tough demands to company business heads, and within a year they had produced major advances in profitability, cash flow, and costs.

When senior executives like Welch and Bossidy convey the message that performance must improve, the recipients of the message become highly motivated. One benefit of such an environment is that the value of a consultant's contributions is multiplied significantly. In fact, one of the most dramatic examples I have observed of effective demand making and its impact on the benefits of consulting occurred in a regulated public utility—an industry not noted for such performance breakthroughs.

Bell Canada's productivity, when this project took place, was about average in comparison to all of the regional telephone companies in North America. For a number of years, every dimension of the business had been growing rapidly, including the number of telephone customers, the number of telephones, and overall telephone use. The size of the workforce was rising equally rapidly. But then, rather suddenly,

there was a dramatic shift: the total workload continued
to rise—even more rapidly than before—but the number
of employees began to decrease. Within a few years, the company's productivity had improved over 30 percent, ranking
Bell Canada among the best companies in the North American telephone industry. The value of these improvements
was more than one-third of the company's net income at
that time, a tidy sum.

What produced this gain? Neither new technology nor labor-
saving machinery was a significant factor. There was no change in
the organization's structure. Productivity-enhancing electronic
switches were yet to come. The key to this turnaround was the
determination of the new executive vice president for operations,
Robert C. Scrivener, who felt that the company could, and therefore should, make substantial productivity gains.

When Scrivener first broached his views to his associates,
they thought that Scrivener, as a new executive, was merely
out to glean some favorable publicity for himself. They were
sure that the idea would blow over fairly soon. They joked
about the "impossible" goals he had established.
    They asked where they could let service deteriorate in
order to achieve the cost reductions Scrivener insisted must
be made. He shocked them when he told them there would be
no degradation of service. Cost improvement would come as a
result of doing things better and faster and doing them right
the first time, not the second or third time. He had to endure
the skepticism, criticism, and even ridicule of his associates.
Yet he stuck to his demands and produced dramatic gains.

One of my associates and I were the consultants who supported
this effort. As we went to various company units to provide help, at
none of them did we receive a brush-off from the implementing
clients like the consultants at the manufacturing plant described

above received. Once it had been made clear that they had no choice but to meet Scrivener's expectations, managers throughout Bell Canada were eager to learn how they could succeed.

This was my first large-scale application of high-impact consulting. While many organizations have the potential to achieve gains as great as or greater than Bell Canada's, very few will ever realize it. The reason is that few managers are willing to endure the interpersonal pressures that are required to communicate high performance-improvement expectations in ways that elicit results. When senior managers make such demands for results convincingly, the implementing clients will be receptive to the help a consultant can offer (as the people at Bell Canada were). When the demands are clear, the consultant does not have to play the missionary role, conveying the power client's desires. Instead the consultant is able to concentrate on being a helpful resource to the implementing clients.

Consulting Projects as Avoidance Mechanisms

Consultants need to sharpen their awareness of how their clients are performing in the area of setting expectations within their organization. They also have to become more sensitive to the reasons managers have so much difficulty in this area. To begin with, conveying high expectations to subordinates can be very risky for managers. For example, by setting very high targets that associates feel are impossible to achieve, a senior manager exposes herself or himself to possible public failure. And the fellowship that most managers enjoy with their people can easily be threatened by making tough demands. Also, when managers set high targets they are subject to challenges they do not have to deal with when they select more modest goals: "Hey, boss, what makes you think such goals are achievable?" "How did you pick those numbers?" "Our toughest competitor doesn't have such high targets, and they have more modern facilities." "If you really believe we can achieve the goals you suggested, how about telling us how it can be done?"

Moreover, by setting very clear and very challenging goals, senior managers put themselves "on the line" to be judged themselves. They place themselves in a position where they will have to deal decisively with people who fail to achieve the targets. Moreover, for a manager to demand performance significantly beyond the organization's norms is a conspicuous step, often subjecting him or her to jokes about their sanity.

Given all these threats to their comfort and security, it is no wonder that only truly exceptional managers dare to demand performance that is well beyond the acceptable standards. Most avoid the confrontations that these tough demands require, and one of the most common escape routes from the unpleasantness associated with tough demand making is the detour into consultant studies, activities, and preparations.

Most sales managers would be very uncomfortable informing a group of salespeople that they will be required to deliver 20 percent greater sales in the next quarter than they did in the last. One good way to avoid (or at least delay) making this sort of demand is to focus on the preparations needed before the people can tackle the goal: "We can't expect them to deliver better results, can we, until we provide them with better training? Of course we can't." "We certainly need to improve the compensation system so that when they sell more they'll be properly rewarded. No doubt about that." "They have said repeatedly they need better intelligence on the competition, so we better make sure we have that available." And on and on. It is so much easier psychologically for managers to undertake the preparations, the gearing up, and the alignment activities than to get on with the job of making improvements happen.

Consultants are frequently unwitting coconspirators in this avoidance game, giving managers plenty of studies, programs, preparations, and wind-up activities that allow them to delay (or completely avoid) making sharp demands. After all, can there be any better way of constructing a preparations-and-activities detour than by engaging a consulting firm or corporate consulting group to do a five- or six-month study? Ironically, after launching such a study, instead of feeling guilty for having delayed real progress, senior managers typically congratulate themselves for having taken decisive action. After all, they rationalize, knowledgeable and experienced consultants are digging into the facts, and they will undoubtedly come up with the right answers.

Most consultants who play this role probably do not see that they are being used as the instruments of delay and avoidance. As they see it, they are providing vital studies and creating essential tools that will be the foundation for progress, when in fact they are providing, however unintentionally, the mechanisms of managerial avoidance. In fact, I am convinced that one of the major attractions of conventional long-cycle-time, labor-intensive consulting is that it permits managers to delay, sometimes indefinitely, the task of communicating to their people their desire for better performance.

Demanding Results Compellingly

As a senior manager, if you ask a consultant to work with your people to achieve an objective but fail to make your expectations clear to the implementing clients in your organization, you force your consultant to become a missionary, as shown in Exhibit 10.1. By contrast, if you commit yourself to achieving measurable results and ask your people to commit themselves too, you effectively block off the consulting study escape route. This does not mean that you will not ask the consultants to do in-depth studies. Nor does it diminish the value and importance of the unique technical inputs consultants can make. What it means is that those inputs will be made in a sharply results-oriented context.

This means that on every consulting project, the senior executive must demand from the implementing clients the kind of tangible, measurable results described in Chapter Four:

- "With the consultant's aid, lay out a plan for increasing inventory turns by 20 percent within three months, and then carry out the plan and achieve those results."

- "Reduce heat losses from furnace 16 by 15 percent by June 30, using whatever help is needed from the consultant."

In high-impact consulting, the focus on achieving some measure of tangible results right from the beginning requires senior managers to convey to those who must get the job done the expectation that they will produce specific, bottom-line results fairly quickly. The message to the implementing clients is neither to make the consultants feel welcome nor to cooperate with them; it is to produce some measurable results.

Early in the contracting process, especially in a new relationship, a consultant needs to assess the ability and willingness of the power client to clarify his or her demands. This is a key dimension of readiness testing. Sometimes consultants will discover that the implementing clients are willing to commit themselves to goals beyond what their senior manager would require of them. If so, go with those. If not, then it is risky to design a project with goals that go much beyond what their superiors are ready to expect and demand. Thus, one cardinal consulting rule should be to tailor consulting projects around the demands the client is ready to make and pursue.

In addition, consultants need to be aware of the fact that this may be a very sensitive area for senior managers. While some managers are open to feedback on their demand-making capabilities, many others would feel threatened or attacked if a consultant were to imply that they have shortcomings in this area. Thus, consultants need to be both focused on the issue of managerial demands and subtle in helping managers deal with it. Exhibit 10.3, at the end of this chapter, provides a questionnaire for senior managers to use in assessing their demand-making characteristics; it could be used as the basis for opening a dialogue between clients and consultants on the subject.

In any event, the aim is to make sure that by one means or another the power client, not the consultant, communicates a demand for results to the implementing clients. It should not be left to the consultant to play the role of communicator ("I know your boss really wants to see this project succeed") or missionary ("This project could save your division several hundred thousand dollars a year"). The ideal relationship between the consultant, the power clients, and the implementing clients is portrayed in Exhibit 10.2.

This relationship was demonstrated quite clearly in the Vitrine Products case, described in Chapter Five. Joe McCray, the manufacturing vice president, asked consultant Harlow Cohen to help the furnace superintendent increase furnace efficiency by a significant amount. When Cohen arrived on the scene, he discovered that the superintendent had quite different expectations. It was only when Cohen encouraged the division's senior managers to be clear about what they expected in the way of performance improvements that he was able to provide effective help to the furnace superintendent.

Strengthening Clients' Demand Making

An important contribution clients should expect from their consultants is help in expanding their own ability to make demands, as Harlow Cohen provided for Vitrine Products. As the initial results-focused projects yield their tangible results, the client manager's

EXHIBIT 10.2. Ideally Directed Demands.

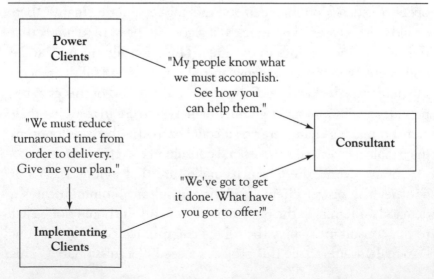

confidence in his ability to sharpen and strengthen his demand making should increase continuously.

There are a number of ways consultants can help clients sharpen their demands during the launching of a new project, even if they are not fully ready to examine their demand-making strengths and shortcomings. Below is a list of ways consultants can help clients in this area. The challenge is to make the steps as easy and workable as possible, so both client and consultant can select and modify the approaches that meet the unique needs of each situation.

1. *Work together on formulating and clarifying the client's demands.*

   Interview the power client about the project. Ask probing questions to help define what he or she should convey to the implementing clients in terms of information, explanations, and demands. Draft your ideas into a working paper.

   Before the project goals are determined, bring together the power client and implementing clients to discuss what must be accomplished in the project. Keep notes and summarize the meeting's conclusions in writing.

   During the process, conduct some informal explorations with various project participants to get their impressions of the possibilities for achieving the project goals. Share these insights with the power client, and discuss their implications for selecting and conveying demands.

2. *Work together to determine how to communicate demands clearly.*

   Help the power client clarify what the implementing clients are to accomplish, and draft a memorandum from the power client to the implementing clients that communicates these demands. Then review and edit the memo with the power client.

   Help the power client frame his or her demands in terms of a range of possible goals; this allows the implementing clients to select, from within that range, the specific goals for their first project.

Help the power client clarify the exact responsibilities of various implementing clients.

Decide with the power client whether it would be better to bring all the key people together and convey his or her expectations to the entire group or to brief one person at a time.

3. *Help the implementing clients as they begin to respond to the power client's demands.*

Arrange a meeting with the responsible people to discuss the implications of the power client's demands.

Help the implementing clients conceive of how to fulfill the project's requirements. Begin to lay out the necessary action steps, and decide how to track and report on progress to the power client. The roles of both client and consultant personnel can be defined as this plan is created.

Conduct a workshop to help the implementing clients brainstorm possible solutions and to provide consultant input on related skills (process redesign, for example).

4. *Develop a process for following up on the power client's demands.*

Decide on the frequency and form of progress reports to be required from the implementing clients.

Help the team to prepare for progress review meetings, to run them, and to analyze what needs to be changed in the way the project is being run.

As with the other checklists presented in this book, neither clients nor consultants should feel burdened or limited by the foregoing list. It is simply a way to stimulate your thinking; the greatest value will accrue as managers and their consultants discuss these issues together and modify the ideas to suit their unique situations.

Redefining Demands When Circumstances Change

When there are personnel changes or reorganizations during the course of a consulting project, client and consultant both need to be sensitive to the need to reexamine how the client's demands are framed.

Take this case, for example, of a consulting project in a large metalworking plant:

> The plant management had laid out a major cost reduction plan. The accounting department was to do the first pilot. The head of accounting, Lee Steig, at first resisted the notion of reducing headcount. But her views changed during a "value-added analysis" carried out in her group. It identified elements of the accounting work that the clients felt were not too important. In participating in that study, Steig became very involved and gradually shifted from being a victim of a cost-reduction effort to taking ownership of the project.
>
> The company's newly recruited controller, Philip Randolph, Lee Steig's boss, came aboard after the project began. He had been so busy that there had been no opportunity for Steig to bring him up to date on the project. The consultant working on the project was operating under the assumption that the executive vice president, the ultimate power client, had filled Randolph in on the project.
>
> When Randolph finally made some time to meet with Steig on the project, the two went over the project in some detail. Steig was eager to get Randolph's approval; Randolph expressed a number of concerns, however, and made a number of suggestions that would materially affect the direction of the project.
>
> Steig was frustrated. She was convinced of the utility of what she had been doing and was hoping the consultant would validate her plans with Randolph. In fact, she wanted the consultant to argue with Randolph; she was very eager to proceed with the plans, despite her boss's concerns.

This project continued moving forward without adequate attention to the changing "client map." There was a new boss, but the same old project was being pushed, without a reality check. When an implementing client is not aware of the need to be responsive to the demands of a new superior, it is the consultant's job to help create this awareness. When a new key player arrives on the scene in the middle of a project, you have to be prepared to start over or at least modify the project's direction.

Another alternative in such circumstances is for the consultant to bring the entire cast of characters together. In the above case, for example, there was a power client, the executive vice president, higher than the new controller in the company hierarchy. When Randolph took over the controller position, the consultant, Steig, or both might have suggested that the executive vice president, Philip Randolph, Lee Steig, and the consultant get together to review the project and discuss how it should advance. Even if that was not done when Randolph joined the company, it could have been done after Steig met with Randolph.

Raising Managers' Consciousness About Making Demands

It would be impossible to estimate the billions of dollars that are wasted each year on consulting projects that depend on a high level of commitment and effort from the members of an organization but never get it due to the senior officers' inability to make the necessary demands in ways that evoke such commitment and effort.

High-impact consulting requires consultants and managers to discuss what demands can reasonably be made and sustained and to design every project so that there is a good match between the power client's demands and the project's requirements. This process will not only raise the odds of success considerably, it will ensure that success on early projects will increase senior management's ability to make demands for subsequent projects.

For clients who would like to examine their demand-making patterns, Exhibit 10.3 provides a self-assessment questionnaire.

After you have filled it out, you might want to talk over the results frankly with your consultant as part of shaping any project you might be working on. And consultants might want to have the senior clients they are working with take a look at the questionnaire and discuss it with them.

EXHIBIT 10.3. Demanding Better Results and Getting Them: A Self-Assessment Exercise for Senior Managers.

Think of one or two recent situations when you asked your people to accomplish something and you were disappointed by the results. Maybe they had a "good explanation" for why it didn't get done; maybe they thought they had responded but really hadn't. Keep these experiences in mind as you fill out the following questionnaire. Use your own definitions of "sometimes" and "too often."

Selecting and Defining Goals

Expectations need to be clearly defined and focused. Accountability must be assigned. There should be a very few top-priority goals. Do you ever

	Never	Some-times	Too Often
1. Establish too many goals?	—	—	—
2. Define expectations in vague or unmeasurable terms?	—	—	—
3. Set target dates too far in the future?	—	—	—
4. Fail to clearly assign accountability for results?	—	—	—
5. Fail to check to make sure the recipient's view of the goal matches your view of the goal?	—	—	—

Negotiating Expectations

Getting people to fully commit to performance targets requires toughness, resiliency, faith, and perseverance.

EXHIBIT 10.3. (*continued*)

	Never	Some-times	Too Often
1. When my people insist "it can't be done," I ease the goals or give them more time.	—	—	—
2. I accept goal trade-offs ("Sure, boss, I can accomplish goal A, but you'll have to forget about goal B").	—	—	—
3. I accept vague agreement ("Sure boss, I'll give it a try").	—	—	—
4. I signal that the goal should be achieved "if possible" (versus saying "it must be achieved").	—	—	—
5. I hear myself offering inducements to get people to do what they should be doing anyhow.	—	—	—

Making Sure Goals Are Actually Achieved

It is necessary to have a work plan, with a timetable, and to review progress regularly.

	Never	Some-times	Too Often
1. I don't insist on written work plans that state how people will achieve their goals.	—	—	—
2. I do not review progress regularly. Mainly I do it when we get near the deadline or when I feel something's going wrong.	—	—	—
3. My people don't really believe that there are significant consequences for success or failure.	—	—	—
4. I do not forcefully confront people when projects go astray.	—	—	—

EXHIBIT 10.3. (*continued*)

Mastering Your Doubts About Asking for Higher Performance

When people don't see how to deliver greater results, they may resist. You need to be sympathetic but also firm in your insistence that it be done.

	Never	Some-times	Too Often
1. I feel very uncomfortable asking people who seem stretched to do even more.	—	—	—
2. Unless I can actually see how a result can be accomplished, I hesitate to ask people to achieve it.	—	—	—
3. I worry that people will quit and go to a competitor.	—	—	—
4. I feel guilty about making my people work under pressure, and so I do some of the work for them.	—	—	—

11

Build Communication Bridges and Overcome Anxiety

As Sigmund Freud described many years ago, certain situations in life create fear and discomfort for no "logical" reason. Starting from earliest childhood, each person develops unique susceptibility to this discomfort, which is known as anxiety.

The symptoms of anxiety are easiest to observe in extreme cases. We all know people who are afraid to fly or who freeze up while taking examinations or who absolutely can't stand being in certain social situations. Those are the extremes, but anxieties afflict us all. The events that spark anxiety in each of us, and our unique methods for coping with or avoiding anxiety, have a profound effect on our work lives, even though we may not be conscious of how it happens.

In this chapter we will see how anxiety patterns, anxiety avoidance, and the techniques clients and consultants employ to minimize anxiety influence the consulting relationship. We will see how anxiety avoidance can trap clients and consultants into perpetuating some of the least successful patterns of conventional consulting.

Anxiety in the Client

When managers engage consultants, they depend on them to provide useful help to achieve organizational goals. (At the very least, they expect the consultant to do no harm.) Such dependence on outside people, especially if they are only slightly known to the client, is a natural anxiety arouser. This anxiety can be exacerbated by the fact that the very act of engaging a consultant—even an internal consultant—can be perceived by fellow managers as a sign of weakness.

The actual arrival of a consulting team can be a very unnerving experience for managers at all levels. Coteries of bright young people descend on the organization with a license to wander and probe. They are certain to discover what is not working well. They will uncover shortcomings in the way managers have been doing their jobs. They will unearth matters that haven't been attended to but should have been. They will shed public light on problems that have been kept in the shadows. All of these possibilities are anxiety arousers.

When the time comes for the consultants to make their recommendations, they may suggest changes that could disrupt comfortable working habits. They may tip the balance in strategic disputes in favor of one side or another. They may make recommendations that will require more time and energy to implement than is available. Client managers will have to follow their recommendations or defend their choice not to. Implementing the consultants' recommendations may require skills and knowledge not abundant among client staff. Individual members of the organization may fear that the consultants will recommend steps that diminish their role or downplay their skills and background.

Further, the consultants may present material with recondite charts and graphs that client people don't fully understand. The consultants' conversations may be sprinkled with unfamiliar technical terms that suggest deep knowledge of the subject under discussion. They will refer to the marvelous things other companies are doing that the client is not doing. They focus on weaknesses and may even convey a hint of disdain when they ask, "You mean your people haven't yet . . . ?"

Also, when consulting reports point to weaknesses in the organization or suggest realignment of tasks, individual managers can feel that the consultants are pointing them out. Consultants may, for example, preface their criticism with slightly condescending remarks like, "Considering the effort that management has been making to overcome their failure to enter this market soon enough, they should not be criticized unduly for . . ." And when there is criticism, it is easy for client mangers to feel that the consultants are taking direct aim at them. They may brood about the possibility that the consultants are conveying criticisms about them to their superiors or to the board of directors.

All of this can provoke anxiety.

Anxiety in the Consultant

It isn't just clients who suffer from anxiety. Because consultants work on the client's premises, away from their own cozy offices; because they are dealing with issues of great significance to the client; because they must deal with conflicting views among different client people and between themselves and their clients; and because their success often depends on the cooperation of people over whom they have no control, management consultants are more subject to anxiety than many other professionals.

In addition, for each consultant there are unique situations that can trigger discomfort. For some it is making public presentations. For others it is confronting "difficult" clients. For still others it is being uncertain of the direction to take in ambiguous situations, or meeting with clients who are very powerful or very affluent, or dealing with clients who refuse to give them sufficient time or help, or coping with clients who get angry or criticize the consulting work, and so forth. For many consultants, the simple act of coming together with a client—any client—can trigger some degree of uneasiness. This anxiety is multiplied in consultants who feel compelled to perpetuate the illusion of omniscience and feel that they must always be prepared to present a brief lecture at any moment, no matter what subject is raised.

Some consultants are made uneasy by the human foibles they discover in client organizations: managers aren't performing as they should; systems are not working properly; groups don't collaborate. The consultant thinks, "How will I ever be able to make something constructive happen here?" For example, in the Electron Digital case that I use as a learning exercise (described in Chapter Nine), the CEO asks the consultant for a training program that appears to be the "wrong" solution. That situation arouses anxiety in almost every consultant who role-plays opposite the CEO in my seminars. Consultants can unwittingly convey resentment or anger about a client's perceived inadequacies, which may make the client more anxious, leading to a mutually reinforcing process that undermines progress.

Clients who feel hostile toward consultants have a variety of techniques for putting consultants in their place. Jokes about consultants, mostly very bad and very old, are repeated—jokes about fees, jokes about bringing the same solution to different clients, jokes about borrowing the client's watch to tell the client the right time. Even though such remarks may stem from clients' own anxieties, they can easily trigger anxiety and defensiveness in consultants.

Storm Warnings: Anxiety at Work

Often behavior on the part of clients or consultants that appears bizarre to others is nothing more than the reaction to intense feelings of anxiety. Here are a few illustrations:

1.   *Leaping to answers*. When clients raise a question, a factual answer is often the right response. Many times, however, a question is simply the client's way of beginning a discussion; the client is not really interested in hearing the consultant's view. The appropriate response in those cases may be a moment of silence, or to ask for the client's view, or to offer a menu of possible answers. But anxiety drives many consultants to provide definitive answers almost automatically, as if the failure to provide one will demonstrate ignorance of the subject.

2.   *Compulsive talking, by both clients and consultants*. Both clients and consultants may express anxiety by talking continuously.

Some years ago in beginning a new assignment I met and interviewed the CEO of a large metropolitan hospital. He said he wanted me to have a good understanding of the situation and began to provide the details. When after two hours he had to leave for another meeting, we made an appointment to continue. After four such meetings, I realized he would never end the interview. It was as if he had an unconscious conviction that nothing bad could happen to him as long as he held the floor and kept talking.

Some consultants also tend toward compulsive talking. Some, in fact, become very impatient when the client talks. They allow the client to talk for a while just to be polite, but they jump in as soon as they can with what they consider to be the real stuff, the consultant's explanations.

3.   *Having a cast-iron front.* Many consultants feel it is important to appear self-assured and knowledgeable. For example, they are reluctant to discuss clearly the limits of their own competence. They will almost never say, "I am not sure" or "I'll want to look that up." Many clients are the same way: they want to appear to know their business thoroughly, and they feel uncomfortable admitting a lack of knowledge or decisiveness. This defensive stance is so common that it can be startling to witness exceptions to it. I still recall one client, who was then chief financial officer of a major commercial airline, describing to me his three key goals at our first meeting twenty years ago. In contrast to the way 99 percent of senior managers behave, he ended the story with a broad smile and this comment: "There's only one trouble, Bob. I don't yet know how the hell to accomplish them."

4.   *Using jargon, and other forms of one-upmanship.* Consultants who feel a bit uneasy often seek reassurance by using jargon and technical language that the client is apt not to understand. Clients do the same thing by referring to their own operations in ways that an outsider couldn't possibly understand. Both clients and consultants can use subtle and not-so-subtle put-downs to gain some sort of upper hand in the psychological duel that characterizes much client-consultant interaction.

Thus, in hundreds of ways, minor and major, all sorts of anxiety-stimulated barriers get in the way of real communication and mutual understanding between clients and consultants. Ironically, one of the appeals of conventional consulting is that its patterns tend to shield the parties from many of these sources of anxiety, but only at the price of having projects carried out with large gaps in mutual understanding. In this chapter we'll examine those dynamics further, because clients pay much too big a price for this psychological "protection."

Hiding Places in the Conventional Model

If one were to design a method of consulting with no other objective in mind than for both client and consultant to avoid anxiety, the method would probably end up looking very much like the conventional consulting model. Let's examine how the conventional model's five frequently fatal flaws serve to shield participants from anxiety:

1. *Defining projects in terms of consultant expertise or products.* Conventional projects are usually defined by the consultant's expert inputs and technical products, so discourse tends to focus on technical or abstract discussion of the consultant's systems and procedures and how the consultant will do the study. Neither client nor consultant has to make any commitments about actual bottom-line achievements. The consultants are happy to delegate the task of achieving results to the client.

Clients can also avoid making any clear commitments to taking action. Once the consultants begin their work, client managers can turn their attention to other matters until the consultant delivers his or her recommendations. Then, if they choose not to take action, they can always call the project a success anyhow because they "got some valuable new insights about the business." Or they can blame the failure to achieve the project's goals on the consultant's shortcomings.

There is no denying that both clients and consultants may feel safer discussing the consultant's research findings and new systems and recommendations than agreeing on a measurable goal and making a public commitment to achieve it. That's how the focus on consultant technology and products rather than client results can protect both parties from anxiety.

2.   *Determining project scope based on the subject to be studied, not client readiness.* In conventional consulting, project scope is based not on what the client can reasonably expect to accomplish but on the kind of technical analysis that the consultant believes should be done. Consultants define projects in terms of the way they view those subjects. So the dialogue tends to focus on factual issues ("How many days of inventory do you carry?" "What sort of delivery times do you promise to customers?"). In this mode, neither client nor consultant venture into important but potentially anxiety-arousing territory such as, "Do your associates share your enthusiasm for this project?" "What have you been doing about this problem until now?" "Do you think you'll be able to get the cooperation of your CEO and the other functions to make these changes?"

As soon as the parties move into an exploration of client readiness, all sorts of sensitive social, psychological, and political issues surface. No wonder this subject is avoided more often than confronted.

3.   *Aiming for one big solution.* In conventional consulting, projects tend to be organized in terms of one big study that will produce one big solution. As discussed earlier, when consultants don't have thorough knowledge about a situation, it feels very risky to speculate about possible directions and launch concrete action. Many client managers feel the same way. They want to dig and analyze and then dig some more until they "have all the data." By gathering all the data, they are convinced, they will avoid wrong moves or recommendations that later turn out to be ill-founded. That's why the large, formulaic study mode is so reassuring to both client and consultant.

Usually the consultants on any given project have already completed dozens of similar projects, so they can follow a tried-and-true process. There is usually a readily available template that lays out the steps. This serves to avoid the anxiety that might be aroused in either their clients or themselves by having to explore creative new possibilities for the project.

Finally, more structure means more control for the consultant, since the template guides and constrains the client's behavior as well as the consultant's. So structured routines and templates that can be modified slightly for each new assignment are an important source of psychological security for consultants. For large firms, these standardized models serve the additional purpose of permitting people to move from job to job and still have them follow the prescribed procedures.

4. *Dividing responsibilities sharply.* The closer consultants get to their clients, the more exposed both may feel. When they work in close collaboration, they fear that their own weaknesses and human frailties may be revealed. Consultants are not nearly as comfortable "thinking out loud" in the presence of clients as they are doing their homework in private and then making well-rehearsed presentations to management.

No wonder people feel safe with the conventional mode of handing responsibility back and forth. There is much less need for open communication in this mode than in a partnership mode. The hand-offs permit consultants to keep their own work separate from the client's activities. The consultants can exercise control over their work, the staffing of assignments, and their work schedule. They do not have to let client people work closely with them, tune in to their thinking, and try to influence the course of events.

The hand-off mode is safe for clients as well. They can sit back, in a somewhat detached manner, and make whatever contributions they care to make, and then evaluate the consultants' efforts.

5. *Making labor-intensive use of consultants.* Finally, conventional consulting makes labor-intensive use of consultants. It is expected that the consultant's team will perform the work and then turn over a finished product to the client. Since the client's people are busy and the consultant is happy to staff up for the job, both are content with the arrangement. In fact, for many clients, the thought

that an army of consultants is attacking the problem at very great expense serves to reassure them that the job will be done well.

———————

There is no doubt that these conventional consulting work patterns provide the structure, distance, academic focus, and avoidance of commitment to results that permit both clients and consultants to minimize their anxiety. But all this safety is earned at a high price: ineffectiveness. High-impact consulting, on the other hand, requires both consultants and clients to come out into the open and take some risks. But the risks are minimal, and the potential benefits are enormous. Below I outline some techniques for breaking through some of the communication and anxiety barriers described above. I also suggest some ways clients and consultants can gain insight into their own counterproductive anxiety-avoidance behavior. There is no doubt that greater awareness of some of these dynamics will help both parties determine how they can work together more effectively. They will be able to experiment with communicating more openly with each other, and they will feel freer to experiment with results-driven approaches. Chapter Twelve continues with suggestions for low-risk ways to venture into high-impact consulting gradually.

———————

Building Communication Bridges

High-impact consulting requires a high level of interaction between client and consultant. To create high-performance client-consultant partnerships that accelerate the pace of change, it is essential that the partners have the best possible understanding of each other. Each of the five major shifts from labor-intensive to high-leverage consulting requires, encourages, and reinforces good communication between clients and consultants.

Here are some of the challenges posed by high-impact consulting in terms of client-consultant communication:

- *Defining projects in terms of specific client goals and results to be achieved.* In order to maximize the likelihood of success, clients and consultants need to explore openly and freely what they might actually accomplish. They need to develop a good mutual understanding of what the goals should be and how much they should shoot for.

- *Basing the scope of each project on client readiness.* The client and consultant must be able to determine together what the client is likely to be able to implement successfully. This requires some careful discussion of what might be possible, what would not work, where is the best place to start, who are the people most likely to produce success, and what are the likely impediments. Rapid-cycle projects that can be accomplished readily need to be created and designed. While there are some slight risks in this process, it can be "loaded for success" so that clients and consultants feel comfortable trying it.

- *Leveraging the consultant's effort by having client people play a significant role in the effort.* Consultants have to be very sensitive about how to best encourage client people to take initiatives. Both parties need to be able to freely explore where the consultant's inputs are needed and where they are not. The goal is to avoid both too much and too little consulting, and both parties have to learn to communicate much more effectively to make this happen.

Expanding the Consultant's Range of Interaction

It is clear that high-impact consulting requires new levels of communication between clients and consultants, but how are these new levels to be reached? Few consultants have received much training in establishing a dialogue with clients, and most do not have any sense of how to improve communication. Consultants assume that interaction with clients is just a matter of talking to them—and they've been practicing *that* all their lives. Most consultants can, in fact, appear to do pretty well at carrying on a dialogue with clients and prospective clients. However, most of what consultants say to their clients tends to fall into three fairly narrow categories:

1. They ask for information.

"Does the average sales per salesperson vary much from region to region?"

"Can you show us how the district offices are organized?"

"How do warehousemen record the removal of an item from inventory?"

"Has the profile of your major customers shifted much in the past few years?"

2. They react to the information and ask for more information.

"So it takes over twelve months on average to bring out a new product? Do you have a chart that shows the process and about how long each step usually takes?"

"You have fourteen different information systems at headquarters and in the various subsidiaries. How compatible are these systems with each other?"

"Eliminating sales calls to your smaller customers has not improved profitability. Where do the extra costs come from?"

3. They tell and sell.

"We think that an analysis of the shifts taking place in the business structure and goals of your key customers would provide the basis for deciding on a new strategy for your key product groups and then . . ."

"There is no doubt that the product-oriented organization which you now have is going to become obsolete as technology diminishes the price spread between plain vanilla and gold-plated products . . ."

"If we were to lay out the entire process from the time an order is called in until the product is shipped and you get paid, we could begin to see what steps can be eliminated and how the process can be speeded up, and then . . ."

Ninety percent or more of what conventional consultants say to clients falls into one of these three categories. These modes of communication keep the conversation in nonthreatening territory, but they also make it impossible to break through the communication walls between clients and consultants.

In order to develop the kind of communication needed in successful high-impact consulting, the three standard modes of consulting interactions described above need to be augmented. The three are all useful. Of course consultants need to seek information and react to it, and they also need to be able to sell ideas. But these are only a small part of the communication repertoire consultants require.

Bridge-Building Modes of Communication

There are a number of modes of client-consultant communication that help break through the barriers between the parties. I categorize these as "bridge-building" modes of communication, because unlike the three standard modes, they help to build bridges of understanding between client and consultant. There are five such interventions. They are powerful modes, but most consultants do not use any of them with any frequency.

1. *Eliciting clients' views and perspective on the issues.* To work in a partnership mode, the consultant must be interested not only in the information clients can provide but also in the views and perspectives of various client people on the subject being studied. The consultant asks the client to share how he or she sees the situation: "What are some of the solutions or approaches you have thought about"? "What are your thoughts about how each of them might contribute to what you are trying to achieve here"? "How do you think the division got into such a situation"?

2. *Helping clients think out loud.* In a partnership, both parties participate in the thinking process. So if the issue is one that the client does not have much confidence about addressing, the consultant can encourage the client to think out loud: "When you consider the various courses of action that are possible, describe the ones that appeal most to you. Don't be constrained at this moment by how workable they seem to be." "How might each of

them play out?" "Describe how each of these approaches might contribute to or interfere with some of the other major programs you have under way here."

3. *Summarizing the client's views and testing the consultant's understanding of them.* To the high-leverage consultant, it is vital to understand the client's perspective. Consultants should take steps in meetings to make sure there is real understanding. One way to do this is to repeat, in their own words, what they have heard the client say. This tests how well the consultant has been hearing what the client was conveying. So in a dialogue with a client, the consultant might say things like, "What I heard you say is . . ." or "So you feel that . . ." In addition, the consultant should periodically test his or her understanding of what the client has said: "Let me see if I can express what you have been driving at. . ." "Am I correct in understanding that you believe the drop in sales can be explained by . . ." "Let me summarize what I've heard you saying and see if I have it correct . . ."

4. *Reacting to how the client* feels *about an issue as well as to its business implications.* The people engaged in a consulting collaboration are human beings, with feelings, likes and dislikes, fear and anger, joy and gratification. These feelings influence both consultant and client behavior. If strong bonds of communication are to be built, the parties will have to recognize and discuss some of these feelings. So, in addition to reacting to the facts and the numbers, the consultant will ask clients how they feel about an issue under discussion and recognize client feelings that have been expressed: "You sound pretty angry that . . ." "I detect some pride in what you were able to accomplish in that new product release." "You sound very disappointed that . . ." Consultants should encourage their clients to express their views about the consultants and the project.

5. *Allowing the client to pause and reflect on the topic.* Sometimes it is useful to keep quiet for ten or fifteen seconds and let the client think. Many consultants have trouble with this one. Most consultants seem to feel that the valuable part of their discussions with clients is when they are expounding on the subject at hand. Some

consultants get so preoccupied with getting their ideas across to their client that they almost hurry the client to finish what he or she is saying so they can get to what they want to tell the client. Competing with the client in this way simply arouses anxiety, whereas allowing some silence permits the conversation to be more thoughtful.

To develop your own perspective on the issues discussed in this chapter, try observing carefully the next few meetings you witness between consultants and clients or potential clients. You'll be able to verify for yourself my assertion that 90 percent or more of the consultant's comments conform to the three "standard categories" of asking for information, reacting to it, and telling and selling. You'll see very little of the five bridge-building modes of communication.

Because most consultants have engaged in conversation all their lives, they assume that they are already well practiced in this "consulting tool" of conversing with the client. In fact, for most consultants who have not been practicing in a high-leverage mode, their conversational patterns may elicit only a fraction of the information needed to design a successful project and may fail to create the basis for a partnership with the client. To make the shift, select just one of the five bridge-building modes, and then practice it deliberately in your next conversation with a client. When you have mastered one, try the next. Gradually you can develop new patterns that work best for you.

Two Additional Strategies for Overcoming Communication Barriers

There are two other techniques consultants can use to improve their communication with clients.

1. *Help clients develop greater insight into their own work patterns.* One valuable contribution consultants can make is to provide feedback

to clients about issues that, while not in the official project contract, are nevertheless significant potential contributors to the
client organization's effectiveness. Consultants can almost always,
for example, see in the style and work modes of the key managers
they are working with behaviors that appear to be self-defeating.
What should they do? If they blurt out their views, they risk alien-
ating the client. If they hold back, they fail to provide uniquely
valuable data.

The key is to develop some ways to share such insights on a low-
risk basis. The easiest way to take the risk out of it is to ask the client
whether he or she would be interested in hearing the feedback:
"After hearing your people talk about it, I have some observations
about how they view the division's new goals. I'd be pleased to share
them with you when you have a few minutes." Client managers will
rarely come right out and say, "No, I don't give a damn about how
they feel." But if they are truly interested in the feedback, they will
make it their business to ask you for it. If they don't really want to
hear it, they will let the matter drop. Be guided by this behavior. If
they do drop it, you may way to try again later. Sometimes it takes a
few tries. Clients who want to learn all they can from those knowledgeable outsiders wandering their halls will have to make it easy
and comfortable for them to share their thoughts.

2.   *Maintain an open dialogue about consultant contributions*.
Gunn Partners, a firm dedicated to high-leverage consulting, makes
it a point to review weekly or even more frequently with the client
the status of the consulting relationship and assess its value. In this
way, work is never carried out merely because it was previously
agreed to in the contract or because the consultant thinks it is a
good idea. The client must continuously manage the relationship
to make sure both parties are doing their best and the investment
in consulting is being rewarded.

Many consultants feel threatened by discussions about the
value of their work and therefore avoid them. In such cases, unfortunately, clients who might have concerns about a project hesitate to voice them until they are ready to explode, because they

quickly recognize that their consultants are really not interested in feedback. If consultants want to stay in touch with how their clients feel about a project, they have to make it easy for clients to let them know.

The Gunn firm is more diligent than most about client feedback on the consulting contribution. For most, the progress assessment work sessions discussed in Chapter Seven offer excellent opportunities for frank dialogue on how the collaboration is working and how it could work better.

Again, the more the client and consultant can share about how they perceive what is happening and how they feel about it, the more likely that the issues that need to be addressed will be addressed.

Establishing Human Contact

In order to produce the most valuable results from their collaboration, clients and consultants need to gradually shift from the structured roles and formalized mechanics of conventional consulting and begin communicating with each other in a much more human fashion.

Both parties need to address the fact that a formal meeting in which the consultant presents so much material that the client cannot absorb it or presents it in a way that frustrates client understanding and inhibits client participation is not a communication process. It is anticommunication.

Consultants will have to experiment with portraying themselves in a manner aimed less at maintaining an image and more at forging a partnership. They will have to admit the limits of their knowledge. They will have to accept the human and therefore somewhat flawed condition of every organization they deal with, including their own. And they will have to search more diligently for (and show more respect for) the knowledge, wisdom, and experience that resides in their clients' organizations. As clients become more comfortable with their consultants, they should be able to open up about what is and isn't working. This will help their consultants focus on the right issues.

Indeed, the ability to overcome the handicaps of anxiety avoidance and to learn to communicate increasingly well is another developmental dimension of the client-consultant adventure. It will not only be more productive and rewarding, it will be much more pleasant.

Self-Diagnosing Anxiety

The questionnaire in Exhibit 11.1, based on one first published in the *Journal of Management Consulting*, offers both clients and consultants a unique opportunity to examine how anxiety may be undermining the effectiveness of their collaborations. The greatest benefits will accrue if clients and consultants either fill it out together or share their answers after they have filled it out.[1]

EXHIBIT 11.1. Anxiety Self-Diagnosis for Clients and Consultants.

Client managers: respond to issues in this column.	Never or Hardly Ever	Often or Too Often	Consultants: respond to issues in this column.

To what extent do you pattern your behavior in interactions so as to minimize anxiety?

1. I keep the conversation to areas I am comfortable with and avoid discussion of areas in which my expertise may be shaky. ☐   ☐ 1. I keep the conversation to areas I am comfortable with and avoid discussion of areas in which my expertise may be shaky.

2. I prefer to work with consultants who are not critical and are easy to work with. ☐   ☐ 2. I tend to pay more attention to client people who are friendly than to those who are hostile or resistant.

EXHIBIT 11.1. (*continued*)

3. I tend to give consultants ☐   ☐ 3. I tend to respond to
   my views quite strongly
   on subjects that I feel
   strongly about—even if
   I don't have strong
   evidence to back me up.

    3. I tend to respond to
   client questions too
   quickly with direct
   answers, rather than
   with speculation,
   questions, probes, or
   silence.

4. I find myself talking ☐   ☐ 4. I probably talk too
   more than I'd like, when
   I should be drawing out
   the consultant's views.

    4. I probably talk too
   much and may be too
   impatient to listen
   carefully to the client.

5. I hesitate to reveal ☐   ☐ 5. I'm not free enough to
   "dirty linen" to
   consultants. I don't
   want them to be able
   to use it against us.

    5. I'm not free enough to
   discuss the limits to my
   range of expertise,
   knowledge, or ability.

6. I sometimes make ☐   ☐ 6. I may subtly highlight
   consulting jokes or
   allude to high fees if the
   consultants are getting
   "too big for their britches."

    6. I may subtly highlight
   client shortcomings as
   a "one-up" technique.

7. I get very irritated if ☐   ☐ 7. I'm too preoccupied
   consultants focus too
   much on our problems
   and don't seem to
   recognize what we have
   accomplished here.

    7. I'm too preoccupied
   with whether the
   client fully appreciates
   my abilities and
   contributions.

8. I prefer to deal with the ☐   ☐ 8. I prefer to deal with
   consultants in structured
   meetings and work
   sessions, to avoid
   losing control.

    8. I prefer to deal with
   client managers,
   especially the higher-
   ups, in structured
   meetings and work
   sessions, to avoid
   losing control.

EXHIBIT 11.1. *(continued)*

Client managers: respond to issues in this column.	Never or Hardly Ever	Often or Too Often	Consultants: respond to issues in this column.

How many of these anxiety "storm signals" do you recognize in yourself?

1. I may give the consultant too big and too global a question to permit an incremental attack on the problems.	☐	☐	1. I like to give my clients big-picture ideas, whether they can absorb them or not.
2. I'm too busy to take enough time to think about project strategies and work plans.	☐	☐	2. I'm too busy to take enough time to think about project strategies and work plans.
3. I may worry too much about dominance or submissiveness when consultants are around.	☐	☐	3. I may worry too much about dominance or submissiveness in client situations.
4. I tend to feel too defensive when the consultant is critical or makes suggestions.	☐	☐	4. I tend to feel too defensive when the client is critical or makes suggestions.
5. I tend to get impatient with the pace at which consultants are able to move ahead.	☐	☐	5. I tend to get impatient with the pace at which clients are able to move ahead.
6. I may ascribe disappointing results to the consultant—and overlook my own shortcomings.	☐	☐	6. I may ascribe disappointing results to the client—and overlook my own shortcomings.

12

Start the Revolution Now: Making the Shift to High-Impact Consulting

Tom Barron, Leader of Dun & Bradstreet's Worldwide Shared Transaction Services, took on the assignment of leading the redesign of the corporation's payroll, general accounting, employee benefits, procurement, and related "back office" operations, which were being performed both at headquarters and in fifteen divisions around the world. The five-year goal was to reduce annual operating expenses by over $50 million while also improving quality and service levels. The consulting firm Gunn Partners was instrumental in helping design and launch the process.

By the end of 1996, the third year of the transition, the annual expense saving actually achieved was $40 million. The cumulative cost of the effort to that point was slightly under $60 million, of which consulting fees were a very small part.

Two years before Dun & Bradstreet launched its effort, Corporation X, with slightly fewer employees than Dun & Bradstreet, brought in one of the "big six" consulting firms to help accomplish an almost identical task. At the end of five years that corporation had not accomplished as much as Dun & Bradstreet had in three years, and according to Barron, they had invested well over $200 million in the effort.

At Dun & Bradstreet, a few Gunn Partners consultants supported a number of interfunctional task teams of client people who did the bulk of the work. At Corporation X, the big six firm sent teams of fifteen to thirty consultants to each location, up to a total of two hundred during the project's early stages, to do the work. As Barron explained it, "Thanks to the training and support provided to our teams by the consultants, plus the experience our people had in doing the work, we now have a tremendous amount of capability built in. At this other corporation, the big six consultants got all the experience, and they'll walk away with it. So the bottom line is that it cost them more three times as much and will probably take twice as long to end up with little in-house process redesign capability."

Although this companywide project was totally unrelated to the Dun & Bradstreet Information Services Division case cited earlier, both of the experiences clearly illustrate the difference between conventional consulting and high-impact consulting. (Gunn Partners calls it "lean consulting.") Over and over, we see that with highly leveraged consulting there are larger immediate results and much more significant, lasting value.

Physician, Heal Thyself!

The management consulting profession is dedicated to helping organizations to replace less effective processes with more effective ones, to accelerate their pace of progress, to become more customer-responsive, to eliminate non-value-added activities, to replace human labor with sophisticated technology, and to face fearlessly the changing realities of the marketplace.

That is indeed a worthwhile set of objectives. And if there ever was an enterprise that desperately needs help in every one of these areas, it is the management consulting profession itself, including all its branches and specialties and both consulting firms and corporate staff consulting groups.

The entire superstructure of the profession is built on an unsupportable foundation: namely, the belief that providing better solutions, better tools, and better ideas about what needs to be done represents the ultimate contribution to organizations. As specified earlier,

- Instead of defining project goals in the customer's terms (such as "reduce costs" or "speed deliveries"), most consultants continue to define them in their own narcissistic terms (such as "install a system" or "recommend a strategy"). Thus they can call their projects "successful," because they deliver the consultant-defined product they promise to deliver, without regard to how much it actually benefits the client.

- Instead of matching project scope to what clients might be able to carry out, most consultants virtually ignore client readiness.

- Instead of carving off rapid-cycle subprojects so they can deliver early payoffs and test the effectiveness of their approach with minimum client investment, most consultants employ a once-around-the track, big-investment, total-systems approach.

- Instead of working in close partnership with clients, with both parties contributing to and learning from the process, most consultants organize projects so that they do the work. Client learning and development take a distinct second place to job efficiency.

- Instead of aiming to empower clients to carry out the project work, thus yielding greater results with fewer consultants, most consultants expand their task definition endlessly. Like Hollywood films of the thirties, many firms feature a few stars and "a supporting cast of thousands." The staffing on many assignments, as with the big six firm in the case cited above, can only be described as grotesque.

All this remains the prevalent pattern in management consulting, despite overwhelming evidence that brilliant ideas about what *ought* to be done come much more easily than the capacity to actually make them happen. And so billions and billions of dollars and millions of staff days and untold months are spent developing great visions about what clients should do and installing tools and systems to allow them do it, with results that are often not worth the client's significant investment in time and money.

When consulting firms believe that clients want or need different kinds of help, they develop new approaches, products, and services, but they almost always preserve rather than reform the labor-intensive conventional paradigm. Consulting firms and internal consulting groups are also constantly developing new practice modes to exploit the latest popular trends. Many corporations, for example, are increasingly concerned with developing their ability to carry out complex change. No problem! Consulting firms with little or no experience helping organizations manage change suddenly sprout a change management practice. Some of these firms have shifted hundreds of people into this specialty; at least one firm claims to have several thousand people in its change management practice and projects rapid additional growth ahead.[1]

Since it takes a number of years of solid experience and extensive coaching to enable even a highly talented consultant to learn to become a skilled change management consultant, one is forced to ask how these firms can recruit or produce them by the hundreds or thousands. The answer, probably, is that they do it the same way they produced thousands of TQM consultants and then thousands of reengineering consultants in similarly short periods.

In a *Business Week* cover story on management consulting, John A. Byrne made this piquant observation on consulting firms' habit of reinventing their offerings and their people: "It's still a little early to know whether the new more engaged and expansive style of consulting will pay off any better than the older, more superficial model did. But even if it turns out to be another disappointment, rest assured that the consultants will cook up something else."[2]

In that same article, Byrne also states that clients are increasingly demanding greater accountability from consultants and more substantial evidence that their consulting investments will lead to measurable results. Perhaps this is so, but from what I have seen the conventional consulting train is running down the conventional track with so much momentum that it will take much more market pressure than has been exerted thus far to slow it down or change its direction.

The Proof Is in the Results

If you are a senior manager and you use either internal management consultants or outside consulting firms, you'll have to deal with this fact: there isn't a shred of doubt that the simple shift away from conventional consulting's five frequently fatal flaws and toward the results focus of high-impact consulting can significantly reduce your risks and increase your returns from consulting investments.

My colleagues and I have been demonstrating this fact and writing about it for thirty years. As described earlier, the high-impact paradigm first took shape in the project that helped Robert C. Scrivener increase Bell Canada's productivity some 30 percent or more. The consulting input there was contributed over several years by two consultants, sometimes augmented by a third, each working about half-time. Since then, we have completed numerous projects that produced similar highly leveraged results.

In each of the cases described in this book, only two or three consultants, generally working part-time, were able to help engage very large numbers of client people in carrying out far-reaching changes. And those cases cited could easily have been replaced by dozens of others.

But it isn't just my firm. Any number of consulting firms, individual consultants, and staff consulting groups throughout the world who practice in a similar highly leveraged mode have experienced similar success. Gunn Partners' success in the Dun & Bradstreet project briefly described above is one good example. The Lexington, Massachusetts, firm of Rath & Strong also works in a high-impact mode. Their projects are frequently defined in client-results terms, because, as described in a company newsletter, "producing measurable success in fairly short order [creates] enthusiasm, which [leads] to additional projects with additional goals." Most of the consulting work is done by client people, with the consultants acting as catalysts and coaches.

The General Systems Company of Pittsfield, Massachusetts, is headed by brothers Val and Donald Feigenbaum, both of whom disdain the label "consultant." Their practice nevertheless exemplifies the high-impact mode. Their staff members work alongside the client's to help produce major advances. The Feigenbaums focus on "quick results." As Don Feigenbaum describes it, "Results become self-generating. When people see it's going to help, it jacks them up to go to the next level."[3]

Rodney Blanckenberg introduced the high-impact approach in South Africa. Amatai and Eva Niv practice in a high-impact mode in Israel. There are numerous others, each of which can document innumerable successes, where success is measured in terms of tangible client returns that are many times the client's investment, with client learning and development as important by-products of the effort.

Gearing Up for Large-Scale Changes

Some consultants who hear about high-impact consulting and rapid-cycle subprojects describe the concept as "picking the low-hanging fruit." This partly accurate oversimplification misses the essential point, however. Yes, rapid-cycle subprojects are aimed at helping client managers achieve some successes quickly. But an important aim of this approach is to demonstrate what clients have to do differently to increase their results. This develops both their confidence and their skill levels. If they merely pick some low-hanging fruit, they will have learned nothing; thus, initial rapid-cycle subprojects must focus on challenging goals that represent a real stretch for participants. They must also be designed to be achievable, however; at the end of the first rapid-cycle subproject, there must be success, a real sense of achievement, some solid learning, and an anticipation about putting the learning to work on more challenging goals. In this way, high-impact consulting helps organizations build a foundation for large-scale strategic change.

By contrast, most who consult on large-scale change, major reengineering, or corporate strategy follow the conventional paradigm's linear train of thought:

- First the consultants lead the client through a process aimed at developing the right vision and the right master plan.
- When the master plan is accepted by senior management, a switch is thrown, and the transformation begins.
- Then there is supposed to be a turbulent period, after which, the theory goes, the organization will be up and running in its new mode.

I call this the "big-leap" model of organizational transformation. As implied throughout this book, however, this model is fatally flawed. The failure rate of these large-scale change processes has been scandalous and the costs ludicrous. A key reason for this high failure rate is that in such large-scale transformations, everyone in the organization must suddenly learn to work differently and to change the way they coordinate with everyone they deal with, all while thousands of related work-method changes are being implemented.

The big-leap model, therefore, places very high demands on organizational members to develop the capacity to make all these changes at once, and yet it makes no provision for this learning to take place. During the many months of the "study" phase, client people learn little or nothing about how to carry out the changes that will eventually be necessary. The consultant learns nothing about how best to help the organization implement the changes successfully. Thus, no matter how much studying, strategizing, master planning, and benchmarking is done, neither party learns much about how to make all the changes work.

In the high-impact mode, large-scale change evolves as an experiential learning process.

Change as a Learning Process

In the high-impact model, organizational learning must grow out of success experiences. A series of rapid-cycle subprojects provide repeated opportunities for clients to hone their individual skills in managing change and coordinating numerous related changes. As its change management capability expands, the client organization can mount increasingly large-scale efforts with low risk and constant pay-offs. In contrast to the big-leap approach, the high-impact consulting mode of large-scale change looks like this:

- First, the consultant helps management quickly sketch how the organization should look after the major change.

- Client and consultant then immediately launch a number of results-focused rapid-cycle subprojects that represent the first steps in carrying out the big transformation. At the same time, they also move ahead with further study to sharpen the details of the master plan.

- Thus, implementation and continued study move forward together. Periodically, the client and consultant use the insights gained from subproject implementation efforts to modify and sharpen the overall strategic plan; these modifications then shape the focus of subsequent subprojects.

Thus management can get moving on major changes rapidly, without long delays, and can learn from their experience as they go. Hamel and Prahalad are two scholars who share our view that in the strategic realm, implementation experience is as important as conceptualization. They point out that in new product marketing, for example, a firm can pursue the conventional approach and pour resources into market research, segmentation, competitor benchmarking, industry analysis, and so forth in an effort to be sure to "get it right" the first time. Alternatively, it can make a series of quick, low-cost, low-risk forays into the market with real products, and learn from their customers' responses. As they put it, "Staking out uncharted territory is a process of successive approximations. . . . What counts is not being right the first time but . . . how fast can a company gather insights into the particular configuration of features, price, and performance that will unlock the market, and how quickly can it recalibrate its product offering. Little is learned in the laboratory or in product-development committee meetings. True learning begins only when a product—imperfect as it may be—is launched."[4]

Motorola's rapid testing of radios for fast-food restaurants, described in Chapter Six, demonstrates the validity of this assertion. Hamel and Prahalad also argue that "strategic intent" is not by itself enough to motivate and sustain change. They insist that the vision must be translated into a series of "clear corporate challenges that focus everyone's attention on the next key advantage or capability to be built."[5]

My firm applies to large-scale change projects the same philosophy that Hamel and Prahalad apply to a new product launch. Both client organization and consultant will learn less from months of thorough analysis and a report thick with brilliant recommendations than they will from setting a few clear goals and acting to reach them successfully, and then learning from the experience.

In high-impact, highly leveraged consulting, there is no limit on speed or scope except the limits imposed by client managers. Subprojects that produce millions of dollars of return on the client's investment within a year or two of start-up can evolve into large-scale strategic change processes, in every kind of business and public and nonprofit agency.

Motorola's Organizational Effectiveness Process is a good example. It was launched in 1984 in order to overcome what CEO Bob Galvin felt was unwarranted self-satisfaction and to get the company moving much more rapidly so it could compete with the best companies in the world. The process created considerable momentum and served as a foundation for the corporation's other improvement thrusts in the late 1980s and early 1990s. I provided the external consulting support, along with a few associates. We worked part-time. We focused on supporting and collaborating closely with Joe Miraglia and his human resources staff. This partnership helped Motorola design, launch, and sustain the process. Similarly, far-reaching strategic and performance changes were supported across the entire corporation by very small numbers of consultants in the General Electric "workout" program. As reported earlier in this book, similar projects have been carried out at General Reinsurance, SmithKline Beecham, and numerous other large, global organizations.

The Dun & Bradstreet Information Services Case: Overall Impact

Dun & Bradstreet's Information Services Division provides an excellent example of how a large number of rapid-cycle projects, used as learning vehicles, can evolve into large-scale strategic change. In Chapters Six and Eight I described the quality-focused effort led by Mike Berkin, who reported that by the end of four years there were $60 to $70 million a year in documented results, with the amount increasing every year. This occurred after an investment of a few hundred thousand dollars in consulting fees and an estimated several million dollars in internal consulting support. But were these savings merely the sum of numerous tactical improvement efforts, or did the effort, driven by rapid-cycle projects, contribute to the fundamental health of the business? I asked Berkin, "You have had thousands of these breakthrough projects, and they have produced huge improvements. What has been the overall impact on the company and on its competitive capability?" He responded as follows:

> There has been a major cultural shift. Managers shifted away from our old culture, where they would tell people not only what had to be done but how they were to do it. Now we tell people what has to be done, and they go about it on their own. In fact, they are taking much more initiative with what needs to be done.

In 1991, the span of control ranged from four to nine people, with an average of about five. Today, there are many managers who have fourteen, fifteen, or sixteen people reporting to them. Because of the shift in people's sense of personal initiative, we have more than doubled the spans of control.

Now when information or complaints or requests come from customers through the "Voice of the Customer" data, it all comes into one place and we send it out to the entire organization. Everybody acts on their own initiative. Nobody has to go out to them and urge them to act on a problem that needs to be corrected.

The whole performance appraisal system has become more disciplined. We use numbers more than impressions of performance. Groups are aligned with each other around common goals. Everyone has become much more focused on results. And that has got us all working on developing better instruments to measure what we are doing and where we have to concentrate. Today, when customer service information comes in, everyone grabs for it to see what they have to do.

During the four years, while our revenues were only up about 5 percent, our operating income was up 38 percent. The modest growth, incidentally, reflects the fact that our new product development effort has only begun to crank up more recently. We anticipate much more rapid growth going forward.

The Unique Role of Internal Consultants

Because (as should be clear to all managers and consultants) large-scale organizational change and the learning associated with it must take place continuously over extended periods of time, internal consultants are in a unique position to exploit high-impact consulting for the benefit of their organization. They have a distinct advantage over consulting firms on this score. In consulting firms, the realities of keeping large groups of consulting professionals gainfully occupied mean that most projects, especially those of larger firms, are scheduled to occur in large spurts. But by having to schedule work that way, firms that deploy large teams of consultants are almost doomed to delivering huge packages of largely indigestible analyses and recommendations at the end of each spurt, in order to justify their fees.

Internals don't have that problem. They remain on the scene, working with their clients over time. They can maintain a dual focus, working on a never-ending succession of rapid-cycle, results-focused subprojects while simultaneously helping their clients design longer-term strategies. The Motorola case illustrates this point. There is no way that the change acceleration process that Bob Galvin was driving would ever have happened without the ongoing catalytic role of Motorola's own internal human resources consultants. While the effort was augmented by external consultants, a major focus of the external consultants' efforts was to help develop and support the internal staff. Joe Miraglia enjoyed close working relationships with senior management in developing and monitoring the overall change effort. And in every sector there were staff consultants who helped generate action—sometimes in collaboration with the outside consultants, sometimes not.

This unique ability of internal consultants to facilitate major change and performance improvement on a continuing basis is an important advantage. It makes it possible for them to play a critical role when they are collaborating with external consultants. They can serve as multipliers who absorb and then disseminate the external consultants' know-how. In Connecticut's worker injury reduction effort, internal consultants played a significant role from the start, and a major aim of the external consultants was to support and develop the internal consultants' capabilities. As the project moved forward, the results obtained by the internal consultants' work expanded rapidly, as did the ratio of internal to external consulting effort.

In the Dun & Bradstreet Information Services case, Mike Berkin valued and made good use of external consulting help, but it is clear that he and his internal group were the critical catalysts in attaining the far-reaching results that were achieved. With a

Mike Berkin in place, a few hundred thousand dollars of external consulting can produce tens of millions of dollars of continuing improvement. Without a Mike Berkin, it is unlikely that even $10 or $20 million spent on external consultants will produce even a fraction of that gain.

Employees who serve in an internal consulting or facilitating role not only make unique and valuable contributions to their organization's change efforts, they also learn invaluable lessons about how to make change happen. For this reason, many organizations assign people whose jobs are not normally internal consultant to serve as facilitators in change efforts. At General Reinsurance, for example, more than seventy-five people throughout the corporation were trained as facilitators to support the company's quality and change management process. These facilitators served part-time as the need arose. Other companies have released such internal facilitators from their regular jobs for periods to enable them to support major changes full-time.

A Message to Clients

As the Dun & Bradstreet experience dramatically demonstrates, you don't have to shift into idle for a few years while you gear up for large-scale change that is always off in the future. The best way to prepare for large-scale change is to get moving at once, to carry out some actual changes rapidly and successfully. Consultants—both internal and external—can learn to work in a results-focused, highly leveraged mode if you insist that they do so. It will be a psychological wrench for you and for them, but it isn't all that complicated. You have to be sold on the importance of your active involvement in and leadership of consulting projects. And you each have to be open to learning how to work with consultants in this new way.

Begin by insisting that your consultants focus on achieving results. This means making sure they are committed on every project to helping you achieve measurable bottom-line benefits. If they say they cannot do this, it means they have doubts about their ability to produce measurable results. And if they have those doubts, you need to ask yourself whether you really want to invest in their project. Insist that they redesign the project until they are comfortable making the results commitment.

To make the shift successfully, it will be important for you and your consultants to develop the ability to divide large jobs into shorter incremental steps. Remember, however, that these steps are not phases of a single project but complete rapid-cycle projects that go from start to finish quickly and achieve measurable results. Your consultants should demonstrate with tens of thousands of dollars of your money that they can produce some significant returns before they ask you to invest hundreds of thousands or millions of dollars.

Insist that your own staff consultants shift toward high-impact consulting as well as any external firm you hire. A number of consulting firms have adopted some of the high-impact techniques described here, and there are many more who would devote energy to learning them if their clients insisted on it. Based on my own firsthand knowledge, I am confident that there are many individual consultants within large firms who would, if they had half the chance, prefer to practice in this mode.

Be reassured that you will not find yourself becoming overly enmeshed in doing the project work yourselves if you move into high-impact consulting. It is almost always possible to find ways to play an appropriate role without adding unreasonably to your workload or your people's. In fact, having to take on more responsibility for your projects with consultants often encourages people to make constructive shifts in their use of time. So don't let busyness get in your way. There is so much to lose (beyond the consultant's large fees) when you simply turn a project over to the consultant and hope for the best. Unless it is purely a matter of outsourcing specialized work, you and your people should play a major role. The jobs will go better. Your people will learn more. And you'll keep the consultants on course. If your consultants cannot or will not learn how to do it, there are many who can and will.

A Message to Consultants

Despite this chapter's title, if you have any interest in the ideas expressed in this book, you do not have to make revolutionary changes all at once. You can began with a few low-risk, low-cost breakthrough projects. The risks are so small and the potential benefits so enormous that you almost owe it to yourself and your clients to try it.

A former associate of mine helped a number of consultants at McKinsey & Company experiment with high-impact consulting, and he collaborated with them on a number of projects. As a clear demonstration of my assertion that most competent conventional consultants who are motivated to do so can make the shift to high-impact consulting, a number of McKinsey consultants have since successfully exploited the approach on their own. In a 1994 article, two of the firm's principals, Jonathan Harris and Warren L. Strickland, described their approach to high-impact consulting as putting small groups of people to work on sharply defined goals to be achieved in six to eight weeks. They described how the approach was used to help an insurance company reduce costs: "The first-wave breakthrough used 65 teams involving 520 team members and 20 facilitators including 5 consultants. By the third wave, the company was launching over 100 teams per wave, using exclusively internal facilitators. In the first year, over 300 breakthrough teams achieved expense reductions and revenue enhancements totaling $60 million."[6]

Five consultants got the effort going, then internal facilitators gradually took over and supported the entire effort with some modest continuing help. In the first year alone, they had $60 million in savings to show for the effort. That is high-impact, highly leveraged consulting. What a far cry from the big six firm that dispatched herds of fifteen to thirty consultants per location in Corporation X, as described at the beginning of this chapter. Harris and Strickland also describe how McKinsey helped an oil company reduce operating costs by $250 million through highly leveraged assistance.

As with all the other cases I've described, no matter how spectacular the measurable benefits from these projects, there are always, in addition, developmental and learning dividends for the client organization. Harris and Strickland assert that the learnings and excitement generated by the initial performance improvements created "an improved environment for other changes" and set the stage for "institutionalizing and locking in continuous performance improvements." They reinforce the notion that when an organization develops increasing competence and confidence in carrying out dozens or hundreds of tangible performance improvements, it creates an environment that permits strategic thinking and action to take place more effectively.

Undoubtedly, your consulting firm has people who can learn to work in this same fashion. As a first step, determine which of the strategies I have been recommending would be easiest for you to adapt and fit most smoothly into the way you have been doing your consulting. Then decide where and how to begin.

Consultants who want to try some of these shifts (assuming their firm supports them) can scout around to find some clients who also might like to try them. You should be frank with clients. Tell them you would like to try a slightly different approach that you think promises better results. Explain the approach and ask if it makes sense to them.

Maybe a good place to begin is a project where some bottom-line results are urgently needed. You are more likely to find client readiness in a situation where management is saying something like, "Our cash flow has suddenly taken a nasty turn downward, and we aren't really sure what to do about it." There is likely to be less readiness when the client is saying something like, "I've been wondering about our organizational structure. We might begin examining over the next year or so whether a more matrixed organization would suit our needs more appropriately." Once you have a client and a project area, you can select one of the rapid-cycle project designs mentioned throughout the book that facilitate the shift to a high-impact mode:

1.   *Performance breakthrough projects*. These are short-term projects targeted at specific performance improvement goals and also designed to test out the consultant's technical or methodological inputs and to provide development experience for client managers and employees. Hundreds of these were carried out in the Dun & Bradstreet Information Services project, for example.

2.   *Strategic breakthrough projects*. These are short-term breakthrough projects that aim to test, quickly and in a low-risk fashion, some major strategic idea rather than to aim at a performance improvement. Motorola's rapid development of a mock-up radio for fast-food restaurants and its informal testing in a few local restaurants is an example of such a strategic breakthrough project.

3.   *Model week projects*. These are projects that ask people to test, for some limited period of time, how well they can do on some key performance variable. United Aluminum's 100 percent on-time shipment project was one example. Vitrine's 7 percent furnace efficiency improvement goal was another.

4.   *Results-focused process redesign projects*. These are projects that carve off one part of a large business process, assemble representatives who are involved in the various steps in this subprocess, and have them map and then redesign the process to achieve some specific improvement goal. The electric utility that was helped to improve its maintenance operations is an example of a client that used this sort of results-focused process redesign. The MVE order entry project is another example. OSHA's complaint-handling projects also illustrate incremental results-focused process redesign. You can carry out such an effort within the framework of a large-scale reengineering project or where a client must improve results that depend on a chain of events involving multiple groups (such as speed of customer payment, inventory, and customer service).

5.   *"Boundary-busting" projects*. These are rapid-cycle projects conducted by a supplier and a customer or among different units

of a single organization who have to coordinate more effectively. The joint planning sessions between GE Lighting's management and General Motors and other customers is an example of how this can be done.

Again, all you need is one or two clients who are willing to try it. You can do it as a frank experiment, in partnership with the client, with the mutual understanding that the intent of the project is to learn how to work together.

An Exciting Future

Once a client and consultant have begun the shift toward highly leveraged, high-impact consulting and enjoyed the shared pleasures of collaborating to achieve some real results, neither will ever want to revert back to the more conventional style. And both will have gained new insights about what to do next.

If you are a client, you will have taken an important step toward liberating yourself from the notion that the experts will solve your problem for you. You will have learned to play an active leadership role in every change project in your organization—even if consultants are involved in a major way.

If you are a consultant, you will have taken a first step in what can be a life-long journey of discovery. You will learn how to be more and more effective in helping organizations accelerate change and improve their performance.

The relationships that develop between clients and consultants can be sustained over time. Each round of projects develops the skills, confidence, and insight of the client and the consultant and expands their capacity to shoot for constantly more ambitious undertakings. Although high-impact consulting aims for the highest possible return from the smallest possible investment, consultants do not have to "work themselves out of a job." The high-impact model requires much less consulting input per project, but it encourages long-lasting client-consultant relationships.

No matter how long you have been locked into the conventional mode, and no matter how uneasy you may be about making the shift to a more multiplicative mode, you can move into it modestly. There is very little up-front investment required. You won't be required to take an oath of loyalty and fealty to high-impact consulting. Nor do you have to renounce the use of large-scale technology when it seems like the best answer to you. All you need—whether you are a client or a consultant—is some belief that what you've read about in this book might work for you. And then try it. Ultimately the marketplace will decide.

Notes

Preface

1. R. H. Schaffer, *Maximizing the Impact of Industrial Engineering* (New York: American Management Association, 1996).

Chapter 2

1. Pittiglio, Rabin, Todd & McGrath, *Productivity Survey* (Mountain View, Calif.: American Electronics Association, 1991).

2. "The Cracks in Quality," *The Economist*, April 18, 1992, pp. 67–68.

3. G. Hall, J. Rosenthal, and J. Wade, "How to Make Reengineering Really Work," *Harvard Business Review*, November-December 1993, pp. 119–131.

4. J. Champy, *Reengineering Management* (New York: HarperBusiness, 1995).

5. "Management's Field of Dreams, Headstones in Management's Graveyard: 50+ Fads and Panaceas in 50+ Years," *Consultants News*, June 1994, p. 4.

6. J. A. Byrne, "Business Fads: What's In and Out," *Business Week*, January 20, 1986, pp. 52–61.

7. N. Nohria and J. D. Berkley, "Whatever Happened to the Take-Charge Manager?" *Harvard Business Review*, January-February 1994, pp. 128–137.

Chapter 3

1. A. N. Turner, *Influencing Clients to Produce Needed Change.* (Harvard Business School Teaching Note). (Boston: HBS Case Services, 1984).

2. For a more detailed discussion of these zest factors see R. H. Schaffer, *The Breakthrough Strategy: Using Short-Term Successes to Build the High Performance Organization* (New York: HarperBusiness, 1988), pp. 52–60.

3. A. N. Turner, *Expert or Facilitator?* (Harvard Business School Teaching Note). (Boston: HBS Case Services, 1983).

4. C. S. Sloane, "A Practitioner's Perspective on University Education for Management Consulting," *MAS Communications*, 6(March) (1982): 23–29.

Chapter 4

1. M. Hammer and J. Champy, *Reengineering the Corporation* (New York: HarperBusiness, 1993).

2. E. M. Mandrish and R. H. Schaffer, "Putting the Engine into Reengineering," *National Productivity Review*, Spring 1996: 7–15.

3. C. Argyris, *Behind the Front Page* (San Francisco: Jossey-Bass, 1974), p. 275.

4. J. Champy, *Reengineering Management* (New York: HarperBusiness, 1995).

5. G. Fuchsberg, "'Visioning' Missions Becomes Its Own Mission," *The Wall Street Journal*, January 7, 1994, p. B1.

Chapter 6

1. D. K. Smith, *Taking Charge of Change* (Reading, Mass.: Addison-Wesley, 1996), pp. 155–156.

2. E. M. Mandrish and R. H. Schaffer, "Putting the Engine into Reengineering," *National Productivity Review*, Spring 1996, pp. 7–15.

Chapter 7

1. C. Argyris, "Double Loop Learning in Organizations," *Harvard Business Review,* September-October 1977, pp. 115–125; C. M. Fiol and M. A. Lyles, "Organizational Learning," *Academy of Management Review,* 10(4): 803–813; D. A. Garvin, "Building a Learning Organization," *Harvard Business Review,* July-August 1993, pp. 78–92; G. P. Huber, "Organizational Learning: The Contributing Processes and the Literatures," *Organization Science,* 2(1): 88–115; B. Levitt and J. G. March, "Organizational Learning," *American Sociological Review, 14* (1988): 319–340; P. Senge, *The Fifth Discipline: The Art and Practice of the Learning Organization* (New York: Doubleday/Currency, 1990).

2. Garvin, "Building a Learning Organization," p. 90.

3. P. Senge, "Leading Learning Organizations," in F. Hesselbein, M. Goldsmith, and R. Beckhard, eds., *The Leader of the Future* (San Francisco: Jossey-Bass, 1996), p. 48.

4. Garvin, "Building a Learning Organization," p. 90.

Chapter 8

1. R. Ashkenas, D. Ulrich, T. Jick, and S. Kerr, *The Boundaryless Organization: Breaking the Chains of Organizational Structure* (San Francisco: Jossey-Bass, 1995); R. Ashkenas, "Beyond the Fads: How Leaders Drive Change with Results," in C. E. Schneier (ed.), *Managing Strategic & Cultural Change in Organizations* (New York: The Human Resource Planning Society, 1995), pp. 33–54.

Chapter 10

1. R. H. Schaffer, "Demand Better Results—And Get Them," *Harvard Business Review,* November-December 1974, pp. 91–98.

Chapter 11

1. R. H. Schaffer and R. N. Ashkenas, "Anxiety: The Consultant's Unwelcome Companion," *Journal of Management Consulting,* 1(2) (1983): 30.

Chapter 12

1. S. Whelehan, "Capturing a Moving Target: Change Management," *Consultants News*, February 1995, pp. 1–3; S. Whelehan, "Leading Players in Change Management," *Consultants News*, March 1995, pp. 4–5.

2. J. A. Byrne, "The Craze for Consultants," *Business Week*, July 25 1994, p. 66.

3. J. A. Byrne, "Never Mind the Buzzwords. Roll Up Your Sleeves," *Business Week*, January 22 1996, p. 84–85.

4. G. Hamel and C. K. Prahalad, *Competing for the Future* (Boston: Harvard Business School Press, 1994), p. 87.

5. *Ibid.*, p. 136.

6. J. Harris and W. L. Strickland, "Achieving Real-Time Performance Improvement Using Breakthrough Teams," in *Property and Casualty Insurance Annual Report* (New York: McKinsey & Company, 1994), pp. 37–49.

Index

learning in, 106–107, 121–123; obstacles to, 113; opportunities for, 110–115; in results focus, 54

Performance improvement: action-oriented approach for, 111–112; and expectations, 172–174; involvement in, 112

Pittiglio, Rabin, Todd & McGrath, 225

PPG Industries, results at, 61

Prahalad, C. K., 212–213, 228

Prasch, K., 104–106, 122

Process, mapping and redesign of, 55, 221

Product development, results for, 57

Profit motive, 63

Projects: assessing, 121–123; boundary-busting, 221–222; breakthrough, 141–142, 221; cast of characters for, 84; defining, 18–19, 30, 34, 45–46, 191–192, 195; hand-off choreography for, 23; labor-intensive, 23–24; large-scale, 21–22, 91–103, 192–193, 210–214; managing, 107–116; model week, 140–141, 221; pilot, 141; in process redesign, 221; rapid-cycle, 87–103; readiness for, 19–21, 67–86; responsibility divided for, 22–23, 193

Q

Quality of Work Life Steering Committee, 53

Quotom Supply, conventional consulting for, 10–12, 13

R

Rabil, F., 115

Randolph, P., 181–182

Rapid-cycle projects: advantages of, 87–103; carving off, 93–103; and contracting, 154–155; criteria for, 90; designing, 89–91; for a dimension, 94; goals focus of, 100–101; in high-impact consulting, 30, 36–37; initial test for, 101–103; and leveraged consulting, 129; and partnerships for learning, 106–107, 108–109, 120; and readiness, 90–91, 99–100; in reengineering, 96–97; and results, 90, 97–98; and success, 103; for a unit, 94–96

Rath & Strong, high-impact consulting by, 209–210

Readiness: aligning project scope with, 67–86; and anxiety, 192, 195; assessing, 70–77; checklist for, 73–76; and client potential, 79–81; comfort with, 76–77; and demands, 177; focus on, 81–83; and leveraged consulting, 129; mapping for, 83–85; and partnership, 110; and rapid cycles, 90–91, 99–100; and success, 85–86; "what if" question for, 77–79

Reassurance, from consultants, 64–65

Reengineering: fad of, 13–14; rapid cycles in, 96–97; and results, 55–57

Resources, and contracting, 155

Responsibility: avoiding, 62–63; divided, 22–23, 193

Results: achieving, 45–66; activities mistaken for, 48–49; beginning with, 49–54; client requirements for, 54–62; demanding, 65–66, 167–185; focus on, 33–35; and high-impact consulting, 27–42, 45–66; importance of focus on, 54; and learning, 117; from leveraged consulting, 126–143; measurable, 142; obstacles to focus on, 62–65; and rapid cycles, 90, 97–98

Retail stores chain, project definition for, 18

Reyneri, N., 129

Risks, avoiding, 63

Roosevelt, F., 27

Rosenthal, J., 13, 225

S

Schaffer, R. H., 225, 226, 227

Schantz, M., 58

Scrivener, R. C., 173–174, 209

Senge, P., 117, 227

Simon & Schuster: in partnership, 124–125; results at, 65–66

Ski instructor metaphor, 89

Skills, developing, 112–113, 133–134, 138

Sloane, C. S., 42, 226

Smith, D. K., 94–96, 136, 226

Smith & Company Formal Wear, and versatility, 157–158

SmithKline Beecham, results at, 57–58, 214

South Africa, results in, 56, 142, 210

Steig, L., 181–182